CLOWN PLAYS

School for Clowns, C

'At last a children's show that is both inventive and original' *Guardian*

The **Clown Plays** are tailor-made for small theatre groups in search of lively material for children. The life of the plays springs from the inventiveness with which the cast can exploit the abundant comic potential of the situations.

Ken Campbell is well known to television audiences for his portrayal of Fred Johnson, Alf Garnett's neighbour in **In Sickness and in Health**. In 1976 he founded the Science Fiction Theatre of Liverpool where he directed two monumental epics: the twenty-two hour cult show **The Warp** and **Illuminatus!**, which was chosen to open the Cottesloe at the National Theatre in London. He also founded the legendary **Ken Campbell's Roadshow**. He is the author of such children's plays as **Old King Cole**, **Skungpoomery** and **Frank 'n' Stein**, plus books for two musicals: **Bendigo** and **Walking Like Geoffrey**. His film scripts have included **Unfair Exchanges**, which starred Julie Walters and **The Madness Museum**, in which Ken Campbell played the Proprietor of the asylum. He toured Britain with his one-man show **Furtive Nudist** (published 1992) and his latest one-man show, **Pigspurt**, premièred at the Riverside Studios, London in March 1992.

also by Ken Campbell

Furtive Nudist

F K Waechter/Ken Campbell

Clown Plays

School for Clowns
Clowns on a School Outing
Peef

cartoons by Eve Stewart

with an introduction by Richard Eyre

Methuen Drama

Methuen Young Drama

This collection first published in Great Britain in 1992 by Methuen Drama, Michelin House, 81 Fulham Road, London SW3 6RB and distributed in the United States of America by HEB Inc, 361 Hanover Street, Portsmouth, New Hampshire, NH 03801 3959.

School for Clowns originally published in German under the title *Schule mit Clowns* by Friedrich Karl Waechter as the fourth volume in the series '3 mal Kindertheater'. Copyright © for the book edition by Verlag Heinrich Ellermann, Munich 1976. Copyright © for the play on stage etc. by Verlag der Autoren, Frankfurt am Main 1975.
Translation copyright © 1977 by Ken Campbell
Clowns on a School Outing copyright © 1992 by Ken Campbell
Peef copyright © 1992 by Ken Campbell

Introduction copyright © 1992 by Richard Eyre
Drawings on cover and inside book copyright © 1992 Eve Stewart

The authors have asserted their moral rights
ISBN 0–413–66550–X

A CIP catalogue record for this book is available from the British Library

Phototypeset by Wilmaset Limited, Wirral
Printed and bound in Great Britain
by Cox & Wyman Ltd, Reading, Berkshire

Caution
All rights whatsoever in these plays are strictly reserved and application for performance etc. should be made, before rehearsals begin. For *School for Clowns* apply to Rosica Colin Ltd, 1 Clareville Grove Mews, London SW7 5AH and for *Clowns on a School Outing* and *Peef* apply to Peters, Fraser & Dunlop Ltd, 503/4 The Chambers, Chelsea Harbour, London SW10 0XF. No performance may be given unless a licence has been obtained.

This paperback is sold subject to the condition that it shall not, by way of trade or otherwise, be lent, resold, hired out or otherwise circulated without the publisher's prior consent in any form of binding or cover other than that in which it is published and without a similar condition including this condition being imposed on the subsequent purchaser.

Contents

Introduction　　vii

School for Clowns　　1

Clowns on a School Outing　　63

Peef　　107

Introduction

I once did a show with Ken at which, in the interval, we overheard someone mutter disconsolately: 'I can't imagine the sort of person who'd enjoy this sort of thing.' I am that sort of person. His work has always appealed to the child in me: anarchic, naughty, irreverent, silly even. Sadly there's precious little work for people like that in the theatre; for children, as they say, of all ages. I mean work that has an innocence, a guilelessness, that is free from the ghastly, glutinous, cloying, knowing, manipulative pall that spreads over most contemporary entertainment.

Most children's theatre appeals to few apart from the managements who make easy money from an acquiescent audience. It's a wasteland, a tundra, populated by a few evangelical writers, opportunistic producers, and dispirited schoolchildren. Worse still is the celebrated English 'art form': the pantomime. Can there be anyone, apart from theatre antiquarians, who actually *enjoy* this pathetic annual parade of self-revealing national bathroom habits – drag acts, fourth rate comics, has-been sportsmen, jokes about jokes about jokes about television, all of it marinated in the basest traditions of English 'variety' (never was a word more inapt).

The *Clown Plays* are something else. They belong to a tradition that is truly funny and truly innocent. If I had to identify this tradition I would name, spontaneously: Lewis Carroll, Buster Keaton, W C Fields, the Marx Brothers, Winnie-the-Pooh, *Wind in the Willows*, Max Wall, Bilko and, oh . . . many more. Few experiences in the theatre have given me as much pleasure as *School for Clowns*, and few performances have matched Ken's performance as Professor Molereasons, the play's protagonist.

School for Clowns started life as a German play for children by Friedrich Karl Waechter. Like many of Ken's most successful projects (or 'capers' as he'd refer to them) he has taken someone else's idea, and turned it into something inimitably his own. Indeed, when it comes to expanding, developing, even appropriating other people's notions, Ken can be positively Shakespearean, if only in his resemblance to Autolycus, the 'snapper-up of unconsidered trifles'.

The play takes place in a (fairly) conventional old-fashioned schoolroom occupied by four pupils – clowns of largely irrelevant ages and sexes, and their teacher Professor Molereasons, a remorseless advocate of discipline. The play's structure is simple: the Professor opens his large book, finds a topic for the lesson (e.g. 'Help! Help! My aeroplane's on fire!'), and instructs the clowns on how to act it out. The clowns always start according to instructions, quiet and submissive. As their invention multiplies and their enthusiasms grow, anarchy invariably brings on the intervention of the increasingly desperate Molereasons: 'SILENCE, CLOWNS!! I AM UNABLE TO CONTINUE IN THESE CONDITIONS!!' His final threat is to leave the room, aware even as he does so of the painful weakness of this sanction. There is no teacher alive, and no child, who would fail to recognise the dilemma.

The play is as fine a metaphor as one can find for teaching, for learning, for the relationship of pupil and teacher, and for the connections between comedy, anarchy, and childhood. When Ken did the play at Nottingham Playhouse, we had just opened Trevor Griffiths' *Comedians*, which, as Ken observed, was *School for Clowns* for grown-ups.

The play ends in total, glorious, unqualified anarchy as the clowns take over the classroom and, with the enthusiastic assistance of the audience, evict their teacher. In performance several hundred schoolchildren would bay for the expulsion of the Professor, who would straighten his wig, a plastic carrot-coloured Mao-style hairpiece that looked as though it had been won in a raffle (in fact not unlike one of the teachers at my daughter's primary school), dust off the chalk from his academic gown, and step down into the auditorium. Not since Christians were thrown to the lions has so much public cruelty been enjoyed by so many.

With great dignity the Professor would process through the rioting schoolchildren, through the foyer, past the box office and into the street, shuffling, broken but still proud, towards the stage door. I interrupted his journey one day, after a morning performance. 'How did it go, Ken?' I said. Professor Molereasons stared back at me with eyes misted by tears. 'I was unable to continue in the conditions . . .'

The two sequels to *School for Clowns* – *Clowns on a School Outing*, and *Peef* – should ideally be performed on the same day by the same actors, in a sort of clownfest. They should, ideally, feature Ken as Professor Molereasons. But perhaps it would be wiser not to let him direct the plays. I once saw a rehearsal of his where an actor who had failed to provide the necessary energy and invention to satisfy Ken was hurled against the wall with the invocation: 'Act proper!'

He once graphically displayed to me the two sides of his character, holding a hand in front of each half of his face in turn: the pirate and the char. The pirate is wild, sometimes savage, sometimes bullying, ambitious, brazen, loud. The char is mournful and melancholic, and sometimes, though not very often, quite tender.

In 1900, in Paris, there was a prize called The Guzmann Prize: 100,000 F for anyone who could communicate with an extraterrestrial being on another planet. The planet Mars was excluded on the grounds that it was too easy to communicate with Martians. I think Ken should, belatedly, be offered this prize. He told me of an encounter he'd had with the Venusian Consul in London; I suspect he was talking about himself. He's been sent here to shake up our ideas about theatre. I think he's still working for them . . .

Richard Eyre
January 1992

School for Clowns

A Play by F K Waechter
Translated by Ken Campbell

School for Clowns was first performed in English by the Unicorn Theatre Company at the Arts Theatre Club, London on 13 December 1975. The cast was as follows:

Weasel	Sylvester McCoy
Puff	Chris Langham
Pimple	Matyelok Gibbs
Drippens	Andy Andrews
Professor Molereasons	Ken Campbell
Mr Bogworth	Duncan Faber

Directed by Nicholas Barter

Designed by Anna Steiner

Music composed and played by Ilona Sekacz

The scene throughout is a classroom

Schule mit Clowns was first performed in German at the Schauspiel, Frankfurt-am-Main on 1 June 1975.

The four clowns were played by Wilfried Elste, Heinz Krähkamp, Ingo Lampe and Barbara Sukowa. Michael Altmann played the Professor.

The play was directed by Hermann Treusch and designed by Christian Steioff.

Act One

Classroom —
Large old-fashioned teacher's desk —
no other furniture —
Cupboard built into wall —
Three entrances: Door L., Door R., and imposing
Double-Door C. —
Enter **Weasel** *Door R. —*
Looks around —
creeps up on Door L. —
opens it and looks out —
No one —
creeps up on Door C. —
opens and looks out —
No one —
lets Door close.

Weasel Everybody's late. Or am I early? No one's here yet. Someone is here. I can see his feet. O it's me.

Weasel *sits on floor, legs out straight, waiting to see if lessons begin —*
they don't —
gets up —
shuffles —
shuffle becomes dance —
finds chalk on teacher's desk —
'smokes' chalk —
finds balloon in pocket —
tries to pull it out —
but it's caught up in his pocket —
he tries to pull out balloon making his leg jerk rhythmically like marionette's —

4 School for Clowns

balloon snaps free.

Weasel Ouch!

Weasel *blows balloon up —*
escaping air makes fart noise —
reprimands balloon —
balloon escapes from his hand —
he studies its flight —
Weasel *makes fart noise and re-enacts balloon flight —*
pulls out another balloon —
blows it up —
ties knot in nozzle —
attempts to throw balloon in air but he's tied it to his finger —
gets it off finger and is holding it with other hand —
attempts to throw balloon in air but has tied it to finger of other hand —
frees balloon and throws it in air —
kicks balloon —
becomes footballer —
World Class —
chalks goalmouth on wall —
(chalked goalmouth extends over cupboard and door) —
chalks circle in middle of floor —
ends of circle don't meet so joins them boldly with straight line —
about to kick-off —
A thought —
picks up balloon and exits Double Door C. —
re-enters as World Class Soccer Star —
acknowledges cheering —
match begins —
Weasel *supplies insane but topical commentary —*

Enter **Puff** *Door R. —*

Act One   5

Weasel *doesn't see him —*
Puff *boggles at* **Weasel** *—*
Puff *boggles generally —*

Enter **Pimple** *(Lady Clown) Door R. —*
Puff, *seeing* **Pimple**, *converts his boggle into look of super-intelligent man who knows what's going on.*

Weasel . . . and he shoots!

Puff (*catching balloon*) But Puff saves brilliantly and boots the ball to Pimple.

Puff *kicks balloon to* **Pimple** *—*
Pimple *picks up balloon.*

Pimple What a thing! Oooo! (*She cuddles balloon.*)

Weasel Hand ball! Penalty! Put your glasses on, Ref!

Pimple I'm cuddling it. Otherwise it won't know I love it.

Enter **Drippens** *timidly Door R. —*
Weasel *jumps on balloon and bursts it —*
Drippens *shrieks and flees through Door R.*

Pimple You frightened him away. What a thing. Oooo.

Puff *delivers his theory on the occurrence in twitty puff language.*

Weasel It was only our balloon. It popped.

No answer from **Drippens**.

Puff Drippens!

Weasel Drippens?

Puff Drippens out there in your pants . . . ?

Pimple Little Dripper . . .

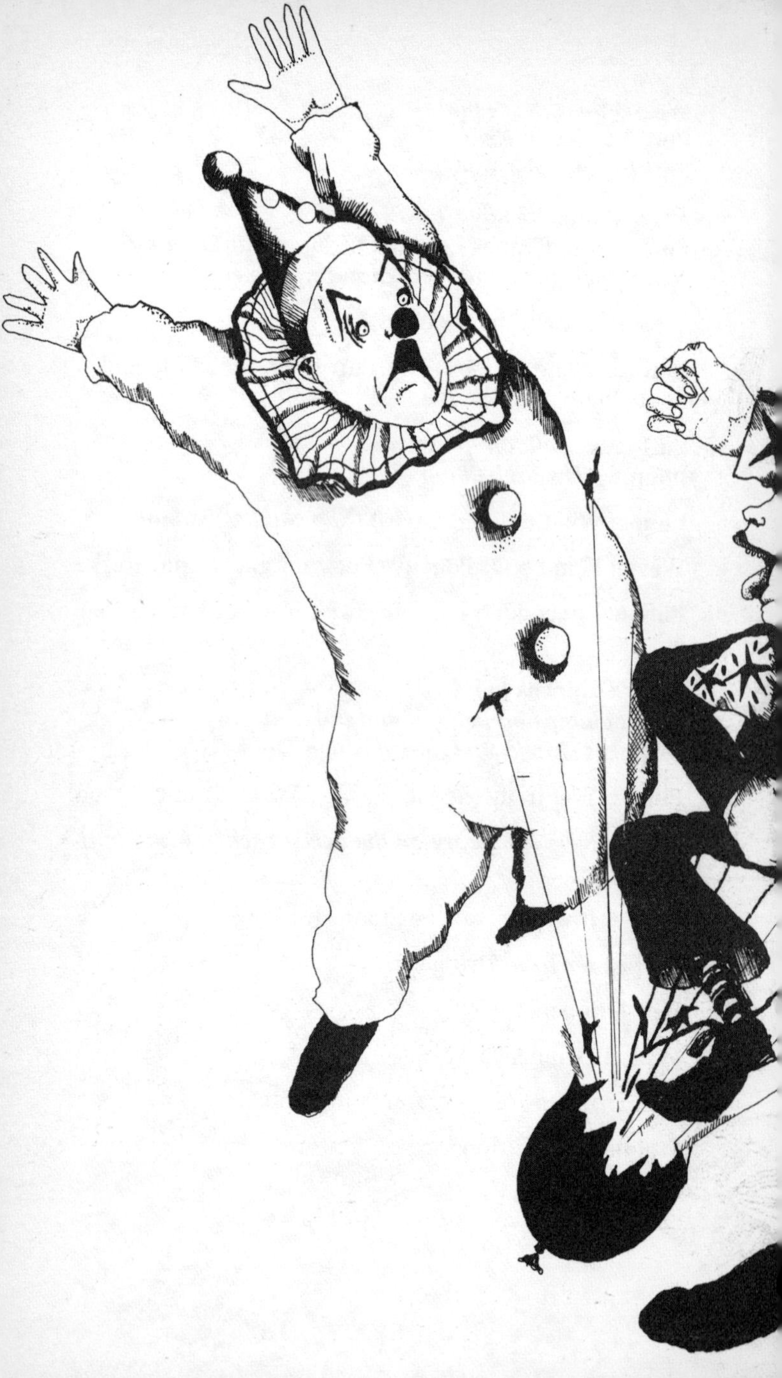

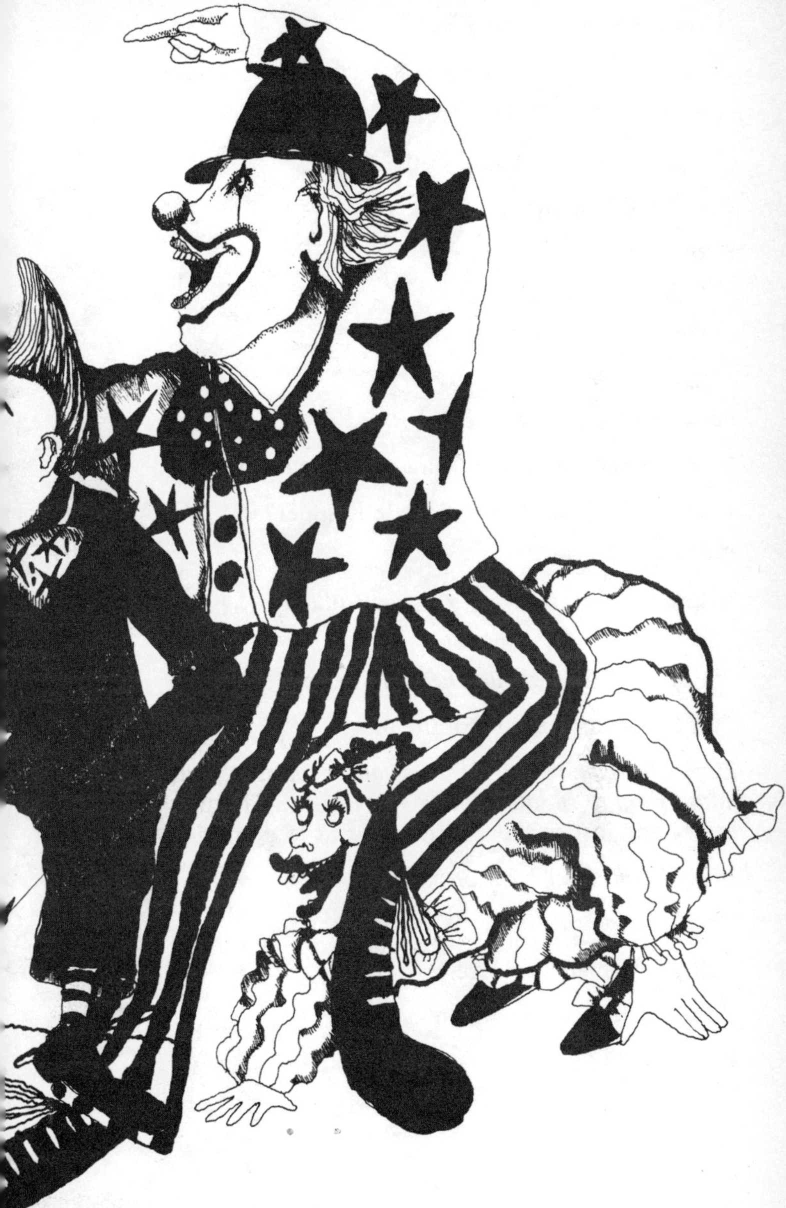

8   School for Clowns

Drippens (*outside door*) Yes?

Pimple You don't have to be scared. What a thing.

Drippens Who all's in there?

Pimple Only Weasel and Puff.

Puff And Pimpole.

Pimple Promise.

Drippens *creeps back in —
looks around fearfully —
sees audience —
shrieks —
flees, bawling, through Door R.*

Puff (*further theories in twitty-puff language*).

Pimple What's the matter, Little Dripper?

Puff In your pants?

Drippens (*outside door*) You were fibbing. What's all those?

Weasel (*pointing at audience*) He means them.

Puff Drippens is scared of them.

Pimple (*stretching out her arms and making off into the auditorium to cuddle the audience*) They're friendly and lovely and just sit there waiting for us to do things.

Weasel *yanks her back on stage.*

Drippens (*outside door*) What are they then?

Puff They're an audience.

Weasel They're naughty ants.

Puff Naughty ants!

Act One 9

Pimple No, they're not naughty ants, they're nice ants.

Puff They're nice ants. In their pants.

Drippens *comes in —*
not fully convinced.

Drippens They're not going to do anything to me, are they? What are you?

The audience's reply (or lack of one) frightens
Drippens —
he exits Door R., bawling.

Puff (*full explanation in puff-twit*).

Weasel What's the matter now, Drippens?

Drippens You were fibbing. They're not ants. They don't know what they are.

Pimple Well, whatever they are, they don't *do* anything.

Weasel Absolutely harmless and friendly. Armless and friendly. Armless and friendly.

Puff Armless and friendly!

Puff *and* **Weasel** *dance the Armless and Friendly Tango —*
Pimple *goes out and re-enters hand in hand with*
Drippens —
she shows him how nice it is in classroom —
Pimple *and* **Drippens** *attempt the tango —*
Drippens *falls into audience.*

Pimple What a thing!

Enter **Professor Molereasons** *Double Door C. —*
with umbrella and enormous book —
Drippens *is scrambling back on stage —*

10 School for Clowns

Molereasons *hangs up umbrella and goes to desk —*
Clowns *race to their places —*
they sit, legs outstretched on floor, looking up at **Molereasons**.

Molereasons Good morning, clowns.

Clowns (**Molereasons** *conducts their response*) Good morning, Professor Molereasons.

Puff (*in tiniest of voices, so that* **Molereasons** *isn't sure if anyone's said anything*) In your pants!

Molereasons *turns to blackboard on wall behind him — writes chapter numbers of the day on blackboard.*

Molereasons Where exactly were we when we left off yesterday?

He is leafing through book —
Clowns *look blank*.

Molereasons Where exactly were we when we left off yesterday?

The **Clowns** *put their heads together in a huddle.*

Molereasons Exactly where?

Pimple Where?

Molereasons Exactly!

Drippens *puts his hand up*.

Molereasons Yes, Drippens, where were we then?

Drippens (*pointing to an exact spot on the floor*) There!

Molereasons Wrong!

Drippens (*pointing to another spot on the floor*) There?

Molereasons Wrong!

Etc., to taste —
Drippens *falls into a heap under* **Molereasons'** *desk and bawls.*

Molereasons Drippens, control yourself, man!

Drippens *bawls louder.*

Molereasons Drippens, control yourself!

Drippens *bawls even louder.*

Molereasons You go too far, you do, Drippens. I am unable to work under these conditions.

Molereasons *waves his stick threateningly.*

If you three don't see to it that Drippens controls himself by the time I return – swish! – whop! – wallop!

Exit **Molereasons** *Double Door C. —
slams it behind him —*
Weasel, **Puff** *and* **Pimple** *try to cheer up* **Drippens** *—*
Drippens *bawls louder —*
Puff *exits Door L. —*
Weasel *and* **Pimple** *exit Door R. —*
Drippens *notices there's no one there —
stops bawling —*
Puff *peeks in Door L. —*
Drippens *sees him, bawls —*
Puff *retires —*
Drippens *stops bawling —*
Weasel *and* **Pimple** *peek in Door R. —*
Drippens *sees them, bawls —*
Weasel *and* **Pimple** *retire —*
Drippens *stops bawling —*
Puff *opens his door and shuts it very quickly —*

12   School for Clowns

Drippens *lets out very short bawl —*
Puff *again opens his door and shuts it very quickly —
another bizarrely brief bawl from* **Drippens** —
Puff *opens and shuts door to Dum-diddle-um-dum dum dum rhythm —*
Drippens *bawls to same rhythm —*
Weasel *and* **Pimple** *open Door R. and cocks a snook at* **Drippens** —
Drippens *cocks a snook back.*

Drippens I mean wah! (*Bawls.*)

Clowns *re-enter laughing at* **Drippens**.

Puff I mean wah!

Drippens *chuckles and gurgles —*
Clowns *idiot about happily —*
Weasel *has an idea.*

Weasel Let's have a look at the book and see exactly where we were up to when we left off yesterday.

*They take the big book from desk and put it on floor — they thumb through it —
Enter* **Molereasons** *Door C. —*
Clowns *dive to places —*
Molereasons *goes to desk.*

Molereasons Where is my book? (*Despite spectacles,* **Molereasons** *has poor eyesight*)

Pimple There!

Molereasons Where is there?

Pimple There is here! (*Hopping on top of book.*)

Clowns *repeat* 'Here!' —
they are in a line —

*they become a train —
at last,* **Molereasons** *sees book.*

Molereasons Ah, here is my book! (*He picks up the book. The* **Clowns** *fall over in a heap*) My precious book.

Molereasons *returns to desk and* **Clowns** *resume their places.* **Molereasons** *decides to launch into Chapter 31.*

Molereasons Chapter thirty-one.

Molereasons Clowns Chapter thirty-one.

Molereasons (*reading*) 'Timothy teaches the baby how to walk. A young girl passes by. She makes eyes at Timothy.' (*To* **Clowns**.) I say, are you paying attention down there, you clowns? Repeat what I just read out – that clown Weasel!

Weasel *jumps up and gives a gross pantomime version of the Timothy saga.*

Molereasons Wrong! I said repeat what I read out.

Weasel *sits down sadly.*

Molereasons That clown talking there – Puff!

Puff *jumps up and stands in Recitation position.*

Puff Chapter thirty-one. Timothy teaches the baby how to walk. A young girl passes by.

Molereasons *is following all this closely in the book. He gives a little grunt at each correct sentence.*

Puff She makes pies for Timothy . . .

Molereasons No! It's 'she makes eyes at Timothy' not 'she makes pies for Timothy'! Once again – properly this time – that lady clown, Pimple!

14 School for Clowns

Pimple *pads to desk and curtsies.*

Pimple Chapter dirty-one! (*The* **Clowns** *laugh.*)

Molereasons Quiet! It's not that funny. Legs straight, Drippens!

Pimple Timothy teaches the baby how to make pie. A young girl buys his pies. She likes his pies, she does. And his puddens. She likes them with gravy.

Molereasons O sit down, Pimple! As I had supposed! Now let us have everyone paying proper attention this time shall we. I shall read it out only this once twice. 'Timothy teaches the baby how to walk. A young girl passes pie' O! – er – all right, settle down – 'A young girl passes by. She makes eyes at Timothy. Timothy is flattered by this and forgets about the baby. The baby crawls off on its own, bumps into a frog and plays with it.' (*He casts the drama.*) Drippens is Timothy, Weasel is the baby, Puff is the young girl and Pimple is the frog. Begin.

Clowns *go into cupboard and rummage out props and costumes —*
Drippens, *now in cap and coat, plonks* **Weasel** *in kiddy pram —*
Weasel *does gross baby impersonation —*
Drippens *turfs* **Weasel** *out of pram and tries to teach him to walk —*
Puff *has equipped himself with enormous balloon bosoms —*
Puff *gives us his 'young girl' —*
He 'makes eyes' with painted ping-pong ball halves —
Molereasons *follows their actions and compares them to the book —*
Molereasons *prompts as necessary —*

Act One 15

*Timothy and the Young Girl get carried away —
they convert Young Girl's enormous bosom into
enormous bottom —*
Molereasons *tries to call halt.*

Molereasons All right, that's quite enough, thank you!
Puff! Drippens! Behave yourselves!

Meanwhile the baby and the frog are snogging.

Molereasons Weasel! Pimple! Get off each other!

Molereasons *pulls them apart with a plop! —*
Weasel *bites* **Molereasons'** *top pocket hanky.*

Molereasons Weasel!

Molereasons *gives his verdict on the drama.*

Molereasons Good in parts. Trifle vulgar in the
concluding moments. Clear away.

Clowns *return stuff to cupboard —*
Molereasons *crosses '31' off list on blackboard —*
Clowns *return to places.*

Molereasons Your undivided attention, please, Class, as
we attack another chapter. Chapter twenty-seven.

Clowns Chapter twenty-seven.

Molereasons Snow White. Three dwarfs creep into the
castle in order to steal the mirror from Snow White's
wicked stepmother. Weasel, Puff and Pimple are the
three dwarfs. Drippens is the wicked stepmother. Begin.

Clowns *go into cupboard —*
Weasel *comes out in jumper over knees and walking
crouching —
he is wearing a red knitted hat with bobble —*
Pimple *and* **Puff** *in similar hats —*

16   School for Clowns

Pimple and **Puff** *have put shoes on knees and are walking on knees with suitcases to hide their legs —*
they perform 'lurking dwarf' scene —
interrupted by sound of shattering glass from cupboard.

Drippens (*in cupboard*) O no!

Molereasons Drippens, you haven't broken that mirror, have you?

Drippens *emerges from cupboard with big mirror frame in which only three little fragments of actual mirror glass remain.*

Drippens Mirror, Mr Molereasons? No.

Molereasons Methinks I heard the unmistakable noise of a Drippens breaking a mirror. If it were to turn out to be broken then I would have to be very angry. It's an exceptionally valuable item, that mirror. Explain, if you will, the sound of shattering glass?

Weasel (*the other three having pushed him forward*) It came over ever so cold in that cupboard and my teeth started shattering.

Molereasons Are we trying to make a monkey out of Sir?

Weasel *nods his head —*
turns to others —
they shake their heads —
he shakes his.

Molereasons Bah! Bring that mirror here to me!

Puff (*quietly to* **Drippens**, *dressing him up as* **Molereasons**, *with jacket, etc, and joke bald head*) Put these on, then he'll think you're what he's seeing in the mirror!

Act One 17

Weasel *puts mirror frame between* **Molereasons** *and* **Drippens** —
Molereasons *'behaves' in front of mirror* —
Drippens *does everything* **Molereasons** *does* —
Molereasons *attempts to touch glass* —
he touches **Drippens'** *finger* —
Molereasons *is almost fooled.*

Molereasons *and* **Drippens** Curious.

Pimple Shhh!

Molereasons *wonders if his ears are playing tricks* —
cleans ears with top pocket hanky —
Drippens *takes other end of hanky to clean his ears* —
Molereasons *breathes on (lack of) glass* —
so does **Drippens** —
they clean it (?) with shared hanky —
Molereasons *spits on (lack of) glass* —
gob lands on **Drippens** —
Drippens *spits back at* **Molereasons** —
Drippens' *spit lands on* **Molereasons** —
Molereasons *molereasons the phenomenon.*

Molereasons My spittle bounced! The mirror is all right. Funny! Heh-hee! I'd thought at first that that exceptionally costly mirror was broken. Carry on!

Molereasons *gives big gesture* —
so does **Drippens** —
Drippens *knocks mirror frame over* **Molereasons** —
Molereasons *bends down to inspect frame* —
Weasel, **Puff** *and* **Pimple** *put on joke bald heads and glasses, becoming* **Molereasons** *clones* —
Molereasons *looks up and sees* **Weasel** *clone* —
backs away —
and into **Molereasons** *clone* **Puff** —

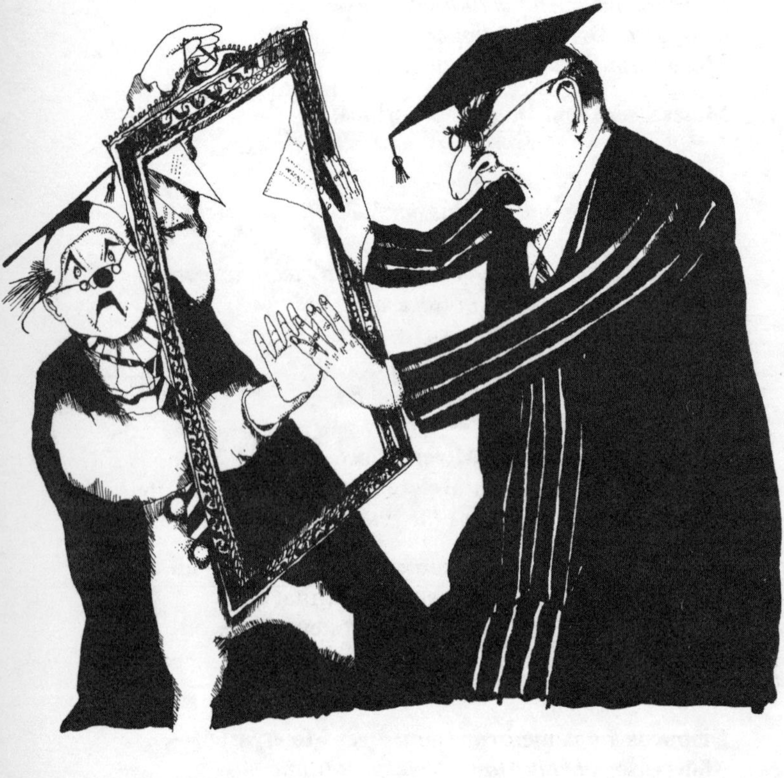

then sees clone **Pimple** —
Exit **Molereasons**, *deranged, through Double Door C.*
Puff *jubilates in twitty-puff.*

Pimple What a thing! Oooo!

Weasel We frighted him out of his wits!

Drippens I think we taught Sir the meaning of fear.

Puff Professor Molereasons in your pants!

Weasel *puts mirror frame back in cupboard —
others clear away dwarf stuff.*

Weasel Sir went cuckoo, didn't he.

Pimple *pads off into audience —
she would like to cuddle the whole audience.*

Puff *reports to* **Weasel** *in twitty-puff that* **Pimple** *is off into the auditorium.*

Weasel (*running after* **Pimple**) Come back, Pimple. We'll get in terrible trouble if we get caught out here in the audimmertoreeum!

Just as **Weasel** *gets her back on stage* **Molereasons** *enters C.*

Molereasons Whatever you're doing – stop it!

Clowns *freeze.*

Molereasons Some order here!

Clowns *shuffle into line.*

Molereasons Some discipline!

Clowns *stand to attention.*

Molereasons Respect!

20   School for Clowns

Clowns *bow to* **Molereasons**.

Molereasons Sit down!

Clowns *sit*.

Molereasons Stand up!

Clowns *stand*.

Molereasons Sit down.

Clowns *sit*.

Molereasons I want to speak to you clowns very seriously indeed. Instances of rudeness and lack of respect have of late been very much on the increase. In fact they have reached such an unprecedented high –

Weasel Hi!

Molereasons – that I am forced, Weasel, into the position of having to administer stern chastisement.

Clowns *huddle in fear —*
Weasel *eats* **Puff**'s *foot —*
Molereasons *enjoys his power.*

You will each come up here in turn and shake Sir by the hand as you solemnly promise to behave from now on in a quiet and orderly fashion.

Clowns *cringe into tangle —*
tangle attempts to undo itself —
Weasel *is released first —*
Weasel *moves slowly towards* **Molereasons** *—*
Molereasons *extends his hand —*
Weasel's *right hand is paralysed —*
with his left he moves it towards **Molereasons**' *hand —*
they are now right hand in right hand.

Act One 21

Weasel I promise to solemnly from now on in a quite orderly manner. I promise.

Molereasons Good boy.

Weasel I promise. I really really do.

Weasel *is now vigorously shaking hands with*
Molereasons —
Pimple *joins in* —
she shakes his left hand.

Pimple And I promise what it is that we've got to promise too. I really promise it.

As they shake away **Drippens** *and* **Puff** *come to join in* —
they shake any available part of **Molereasons'** *person* —
Molereasons *caves in under pressure of promises and*
Clowns *pile up on top of him.*

Molereasons (*from the bottom of the clown heap. Matter of factly, as if at his desk*) This is your idea of discipline, is it?

Puff It just seemed to happen.

Molereasons This is order, as you see it?

Weasel We were just a bit on the keen side perhaps.

Molereasons This is you showing respect, is it?

Pimple You can never know what you're poohing till you've dung it.

Molereasons (*bellowing*) You are lying on your teach-ah!

Clowns *spring up and flit angelically to places* —
Molereasons' *leg is twisted* —
he straightens it painfully with his stick —
Molereasons *is moved by angelic faces of* **Clowns**.

22   School for Clowns

Molereasons You all mean well. I know that. It's just that your ever-tempestuous, effervescent temperaments are your enemies within. Well we must all fight against our enemies. Do Battle with 'em. I want you, from this moment on, to declare war on your weaknesses.

Weasel (*brandishing imaginary sword*) War on your weaknesses!

Others (*all brandishing imaginary swords*) Hurray! War!

Clowns *dive into cupboard and emerge equipped for war —*
they fight enthusiastically —
the wounded are tied up in immense lengths of bandage —
Molereasons *cowers behind desk —*
Bandage festoons the classroom —
Clowns *freeze in heroic war pose —*
it's clear they think they have done well.

Molereasons Well, thank you very much, class, for a very excellent example of EXACTLY WHAT I DIDN'T MEAN!!! By war, I mean paying proper attention to me when I'm reading from the book! By war, I mean discipline! This is a mouth and not a noise-hole.

Clowns *bundle war gear back into cupboard —*
Puff, **Pimple** *and* **Drippens** *take up places —*
Weasel *is still in cupboard getting off bandage.*

Molereasons Where's that clown, Weasel?

Weasel *sitting on a bit of wood with little castors on it trundles neatly into place.*

Molereasons I shall now read another chapter. Let's have every single clown giving me his/her full attention. Showing me that you've understood what we mean by war in this sense. Chapter fifty-six. Help. My aeroplane's on fire.

Pimple *springs up to help* **Molereasons** —
she looks for aeroplane.

Molereasons 'Chapter fifty-six. Help. My aeroplane's on fire.' Sit down, Pimple, please. (*She sits.*) 'Three men are sitting round a pond . . .'

Molereasons *leaves the desk and chalks a circle round himself on the floor —*
he jumps out of the 'pond' and bounds surprisingly athletically to the desk —
he recaps.

Molereasons '. . . men are sitting round a pond fishing. An aeroplane streaks across the skies. It is on fire. The Pilot shrieks out "Help!" '

Weasel (*to* **Pimple** *who is getting up again*) His aeroplane's on fire.

Molereasons Thank you. 'And he buckles on his parachute and launches himself into space. He lands right in the middle of the pond. The splash frightens all the fishes away and the Pilot is very ashamed of himself for having spoilt the anglers' fun.' Pimple, Drippens and Weasel are the three anglers. Puff is the Pilot. Begin.

Anglers get rods, lines, fishes out of cupboard —
Weasel*'s line is elastic with something rude on the end —*
he whangs it everywhere, including at the audience —
Molereasons *stops him and sits him round the 'pond' —*
Pimple *pads into the audience.*

Molereasons Audience participation is not on our curriculum, Pimple.

Guides her back on stage —
Drippens *is kissing his fish.*

Molereasons Round the pond, Drippens, please.

Puff *is on top of the cupboard with a large toy plane.*

Molereasons 'Three men are sitting round a pond fishing' . . . good . . . string end of rod goes in pond, Pimple. 'An aeroplane streaks across the skies . . .'

Puff *gets hold of rope —*
dithers —
launches off with toy plane —
swings across stage on rope.

Puff Streakeeee-poo!

Molereasons *throws a lighted match at the plane.*

Molereasons It is on fire!

Puff Help! My aeroplane's on fire!

Puff *throws plane on floor —*
lets go of rope —
lands beside 'pond' —
immense parachute follows him down.

Molereasons Parachute . . . good. Get right in the middle of the pond, Puff. He lands right in the middle of the pond.

Puff *jumps into 'pond' —*
spits out jet of water which lands on **Molereasons**' *head —*
Molereasons *looks at ceiling, suspecting a leak.*

Molereasons I've told Mr Bogworth about that roof. (*To* **Puff**.) And now the splash frightens all the fishes away.

Puff (*picking up the fish and tossing them into the air*) Splash – splasher – splashest!

Drippens *goes to fish he was kissing —*
gets little doll's bed out of cupboard and tucks fish up in it —
fish dies —
Drippens *listens for fishy heartbeat —*
covers fish's head with sheet.

Molereasons . . . and the Pilot is very ashamed of himself, he has spoilt the anglers' fun. Go on, be very ashamed of yourself, Puff.

Puff *exhibits shame —*
sinks at knees and grovels —
blows nose on parachute —
Molereasons *is pleased by display —*
Molereasons *goes to blackboard to give this chapter a tick —*
Puff *discovers new world under parachute —*
Pimple, **Weasel** *and* **Drippens** *join him under parachute —*
Molereasons *about to start next chapter —*
Molereasons *sees squirming shapes under parachute.*

Molereasons All right, thank you.

The parachute becomes like an arctic tent with the four clowns' faces at the central hole.

Molereasons Puff, Weasel, Pimple, Drippens! Out of there. Out you come.

The **Clowns** *experiment with the flow of the parachute.*

Molereasons I don't know whether you clowns have got cloth ears or what, but I told you to get out of that parachute!

26 School for Clowns

Clowns *and parachute become a whale —*
central hole of parachute is mouth —
Mouth sings 'Mammy'.

Thank you very much – now just get out!

Whale turns into chomping shark —
Shark eats **Molereasons**, *stick and all —*
becomes a hippo and shits out **Molereasons** —
Hippo turns and belches out stick —
Molereasons *picks up stick and threatens the* **Clowns** *still under parachute.*

Molereasons Come along now. This silliness has gone on quite long enough. (*Aside.*) Idea. (*Aloud.*) I am unable to work under these conditions! Slam!

Molereasons *slams the Double Door C., but stays in classroom —*
he creeps to desk and hides behind —
Clowns *emerge from parachute, laughing.*

Molereasons (*suddenly manifesting himself at his desk*) Chapter thirty-four!

Clowns (*sitting down flabbergasted*) Chapter thirty-four.

Molereasons (*reading*) 'The dying idiot. An old idiot lies on the point of death. He calls his three sons to his bedside and addresses them thus:'

Molereasons *suddenly notices that the* **Clowns** *have gone back under the parachute.*

Molereasons Well, if I can't educate the top end of a clown I shall attempt to educate the bottom.

Molereasons *runs at* **Clowns** *with stick —*
parachute, like a bull, jumps out of the way —
Molereasons *takes another run at them —*

Act One   27

'bull' dodges —
Molereasons *hurtles out of Door L. —*
sound of crash —
Clowns *emerge from under parachute —*
they look out of Door L.

Puff He's fallen down stairs!

Weasel Hey!

Weasel *goes to cupboard and gets out large cushion and stuffs it under parachute —*
effect is of someone under parachute —
Pimple, **Puff** *and* **Drippens** *are impressed —*
they get cushions and bolster and put them under parachute —
Weasel *is worried about the audience, so he speaks to them.*

Weasel Listen, don't give us away, will you, and if anyone in the next seat to you starts to give us away – thump 'im! (*Looking out of Door L.*) He's coming!

The **Clowns** *hide behind the cupboard —*
Re-enter **Molereasons** *—*
he has crashed through a portrait which is round his neck —
he takes it off and tosses it away —
he sees the shape of **Clowns** *under parachute —*
he wallops cushions with stick —
ferociously —
exhausted, he stops —
he notes no movement from under parachute.

Molereasons What have I done? Hello? Can you hear me? I'm sorry. I really am sorry – look! (*He throws his stick away.*) Was it a bit hard, was it? Why are you so quiet? It really did hurt you, did it? Please say

28   School for Clowns

something. O my God, I've done them in! Oh clowns! – the thing is I need you!

Unseen by **Molereasons** *the* **Clowns** *creep back to their places.*

Molereasons There have been times when I've been wrong. There have only been times when I've been wrong. O Lord in the Sky only bring those dear clowns back to life again and I promise I will deal with their delightful if somewhat effervescent personalities (*Sees the* **Clowns** *but without fully taking in the sight.*) – Good Morning – with love and understanding.

Molereasons *boggles at the* **Clowns** *and then at the heap and then at the* **Clowns** *and then at the heap.*

Molereasons It is you! It is you!

Weasel We all fall down!

*And they do —
with the emotional* **Molereasons** *on top of them.*

Molereasons O clowns! Clowns! You just gave me a terrifying shock there. But I'm hopeful that it may have done me good, this shock. I hope I may be able to learn from it. You know what I'm going to try now? – I'm going to try these brand new teaching techniques. No Book. You are all now free to be yourselves. You can now do anything you like. Whatever you do is right. I don't stop you from doing anything. All I do is just keep very still and quiet in my corner and watch what you do and love it. Begin.

Clowns *get up uncertainly —
they brood —
one whistles —
one half-heartedly waggles his ears —*

Act One 29

sudden snatch of song —
Nothing comes to anything —
Everything comes to nothing —
Sadly, sulkily, they clear the props into the cupboard.

Molereasons Er Weasel – I don't want to interfere with your self-expression in any way – but what's the matter?

Weasel We don't know what to do.

Pimple We don't know how to what.

Drippens We don't know where to how.

Molereasons (*attempting humour*) I say, it's like now that you can do anything you want to you don't want to do anything!

Drippens *bursts into tears —*
one by one the others weep noisily —
Drippens *sprays cast and audience with his squirting tears.*

Molereasons O no! Please! Look I am unable to work under these conditions! So they don't work either, these wonderful new soft teaching techniques! I'll tell you what teaching's all about – it's about being hard! Being tough! Everything according to the book! It's about manners! Respect! Obedience! Well-bred behaviour! Fine ideals! Decorum! And above all – (*Important looking doorknob in hand.*) harsh discipline! (*Exits like thunder.*)

Clowns *jump for joy —*
(*all they needed for full happiness was the absence of* **Molereasons**) —
Puff *puts on pair of spectacles, making him look like* **Molereasons** —

he slams the Double Door C. in the **Molereasons** *manner —*
Weasel, **Drippens** *and* **Pimple** *dive for their places.*

Puff (*impersonating* **Molereasons**) I am Professor Molereasons. And I live in a holereasons. Your undivided attention please, class, as we attack another chapter. That clown Weasel, down there in your pants, repeat what I just read out.

Weasel *gets up —*
he can't remember **Puff** *having read anything out —*
he dithers —
he sits.

Puff As I had supposed. Let us have everyone paying full attention, shall we. I shall read this out only twice once! 'Chapter seventy-seven.'

The Others Chapter seventy-seven!

Puff The wooing.

Others The wooing.

Puff The woo- - -ing!

Others The woo- - -ing!

Puff The woo-yihihing!

Others The woo-yihihing!

Puff (*pretending to read*) Sir Lancelump loves Lady Goonerviere. Lady Goonerviere lives at the top of a large tower. Weasel is Sir Lancelump. Pimple is Lady Goonerviere and Drippens is the Tower. Begin!

Clowns *go into cupboard —*
Drippens *comes out with huge tube of cloth —*
he sticks **Molereasons**' *umbrella up the tube of cloth —*

Act One   31

the effect is of a tower —
Pimple *goes into 'tower' and climbs on* **Drippens'** *shoulders —*
she cuts a 'window' in 'tower' with scissors —
Puff *whispers something in her ear —*
she titters —
Puff *gives her bucket of flour —*
Pimple *tries to move her lips to* **Drippens'** *voice.*

Drippens If only a dashing young man would come and tirra-lirra me with his lute and declare his love for me.

Weasel *comes out of cupboard in knight's helmet —*
he unrolls red carpet in front of 'tower' —
Lady Goonerviere primps and poses.

Weasel What a beautiful pale skin you've got.

Pimple Well, tirra-lirra me then.

Weasel *looks lost.*

Puff Serenade the lady, Weasel.

Weasel *produces large comb —*
combs plumes of helmet —
produces sandwich wrapped in tissue paper —
tosses sandwich away and wraps tissue round comb and serenades —
Pimple *pours flour on his head and hurls bucket at him —*

Weasel *goes to throw bucket at her —*

Puff *cautions him.*

Puff Weasel!

Weasel Well, if I can't kiss your beautiful pale skin I shall kiss your beautiful pail!

Weasel *kisses bucket —*

32 School for Clowns

beats out rhythm on bucket —
Puff *pulls him off-stage on carpet, Door L. —*
Weasel *pops his head round Door.*

All right, this time I'm really going to impress you!
(*Pops back out to ready himself.*)

Puff (*brandishing scissors*) I am Professor Molereasons
and I live in a holereasons. On my fire I put coalreasons.
I don't like football because I can't see the goalreasons.
My favourite music is Rock and Rollreasons. And when
I die up to Heaven will go my soulreasons.

Enter **Weasel** *on roller-skates strumming ukulele —*
Puff *snips* **Weasel**'s *braces with scissors —*
Weasel *tap-dances on skates singing 'Sheik of Araby' —*
Drippens, **Pimple** *and* **Puff** *sing 'ain't got no pants on' as
line by line refrain —*
Weasel's *pants come down —*
the 'tower' dances to the music —
Weasel *notes his pantlessness —*
seeks to hide confusion behind ukulele —
Weasel *exits Door L. —*
his head pops round.

Weasel This time I'm really going to impress you, you
fascinatin' witch!

Puff *has an idea and hands a witch mask and rose to*
Pimple.

Puff Hurry up Weasel out there in your pants. Or rather,
not in your pants. I am unable to work under these
conditions. I am unable to lurk under these conditions. I
am unable to Turk under these conditions and I am
unable to jerk under these conditions and I am unable to
perk under these conditions and I am unable to quirk

under these conditions and I am unable to murk under these conditions.

Weasel *roars into classroom on motorbike —
does flashy circuit with tricks —
halts beneath 'tower' —
serenades Lady Goonerviere on toy sax —
hoots his hooter —
revs —
and all to a Strauss waltz! —
Lady Goonerviere throws him a rose.*

Weasel A rose! Lady Goonerviere loves me! (*The rose squirts him in the face.*)

Pimple *moves her lips to* **Drippens**' *voice.*

Drippens Yes, I love you and I come to you.

Pimple *collapses the umbrella and the tower of cloth and now appears (still on* **Drippens**' *shoulders) as a hideous giant witch woman —*
Weasel *is terrified —
he kicks the motorbike into gear and is about to roar out through Double Door C., but is confronted by the returning* **Molereasons** —
Weasel *turns the motorbike away —
but again faces witch-woman —
panic —*
Molereasons *chases him —*
Molereasons *catches hold of strap on back of motorbike —*
Molereasons *falls on his back and* **Weasel** *drives them both through the classroom wall —
bricks, plaster and filth fly —*
Molereasons *re-enters through hole in wall —
he is coughing and sneezing.*

34 School for Clowns

Molereasons I just go out for two minutes and look what happens! Let's have some order here! Some quiet! Some discipline!

Drippens *is building up to a big sneeze.*

Don't sneeze!

Drippens *is about to bawl.*

And don't bawl.

Weasel *returns through hole in wall —
there is a brick stuck in his helmet —
an exhaust pipe in his socks.*

A public apology for this outrage – Puff!

Puff (*still impersonating* **Molereasons**) A public apology for this outrage – Puff!

Molereasons Bah!

Molereasons *tries to strike* **Puff** *but he brains the already dizzy* **Weasel**.

Molereasons A public apology begins with the word 'Sir'. Once again, properly this time – Weasel doesn't seem quite up to it – the lady clown, Pimple.

Pimple *goes up to* **Molereasons**' *desk, curtsies and says.*

Pimple Dear Professor Molereasons Sir. We wish to make it clear that we are extremely sorry for the outrage, and it was an outrage, and that's why you're inraged because we outraged, and we won't do it ever again, if only you Sir, in your big mercy could just forgive us, just this once . . . oh, go on, Sir . . . and we will be good for ever and always. Amen.

Act One 35

Pimple *has nervously fiddled a button of her outfit into button hole of* **Molereasons'** *jacket.*

Molereasons Good. Thank you. Chapter thirty-four.

Clowns Chapter thirty-four.

Molereasons (*reading*) 'The dying idiot. An old idiot lies on the point of death. He calls his three sons to his bedside and addresses them thus . . .' (**Molereasons** *is suddenly aware of* **Pimple** *fiddling with his jacket button.*) Pimple, go and sit down! What on earth are you at, woman? Are you asking to have your head squeezed? This is a continuing naughtiness while Sir is actually trying to read from the book.

Pimple *divests herself of the upper part of her outfit —
it dangles from* **Molereasons'** *jacket buttonhole —
she takes her place.*

A naughtiness of that order deserves severe chastisement!

Molereasons *strides towards* **Pimple** *but trips over the bit of her outfit still dangling from button —
his book flies out of his hands —
he knocks himself out on the floor.*

Pimple What a thing! Eh? Ooo.

Drippens Bad luck there, Sir!

Weasel Poor old Sir!

Clowns *try to get* **Molereasons** *up —
on his head —
drop him —
on his feet —
he falls forward —
they catch him —*

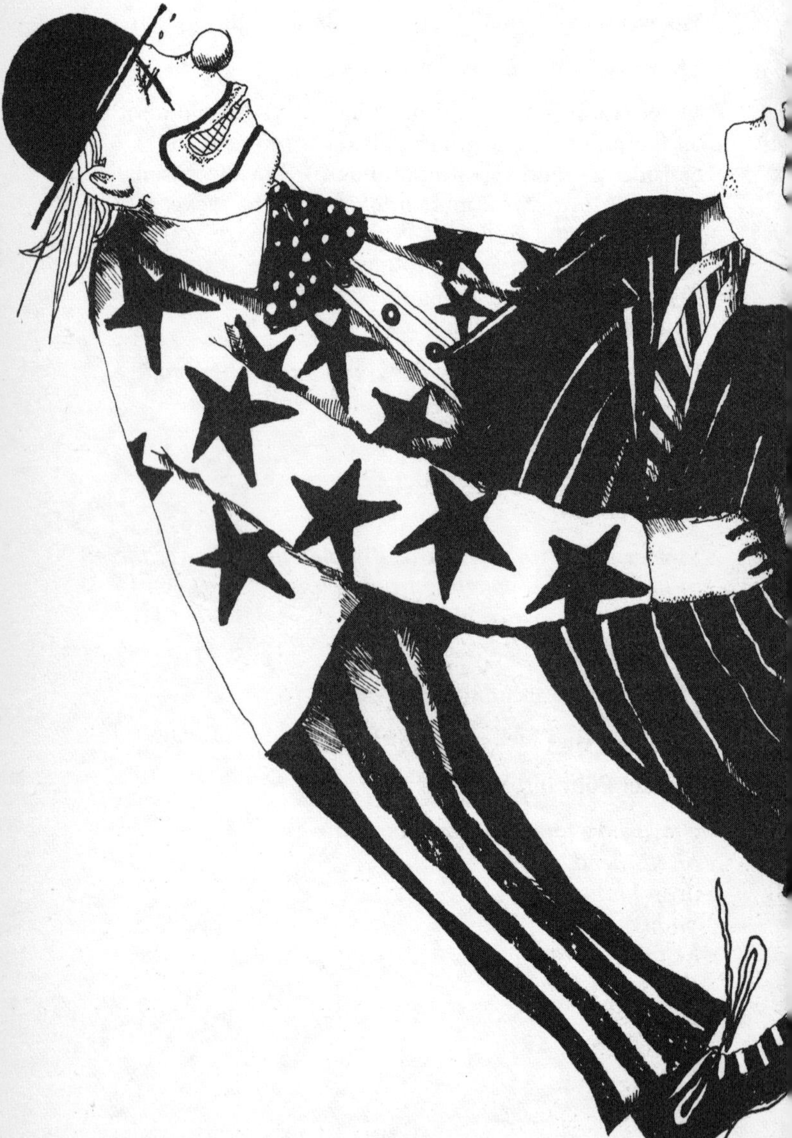

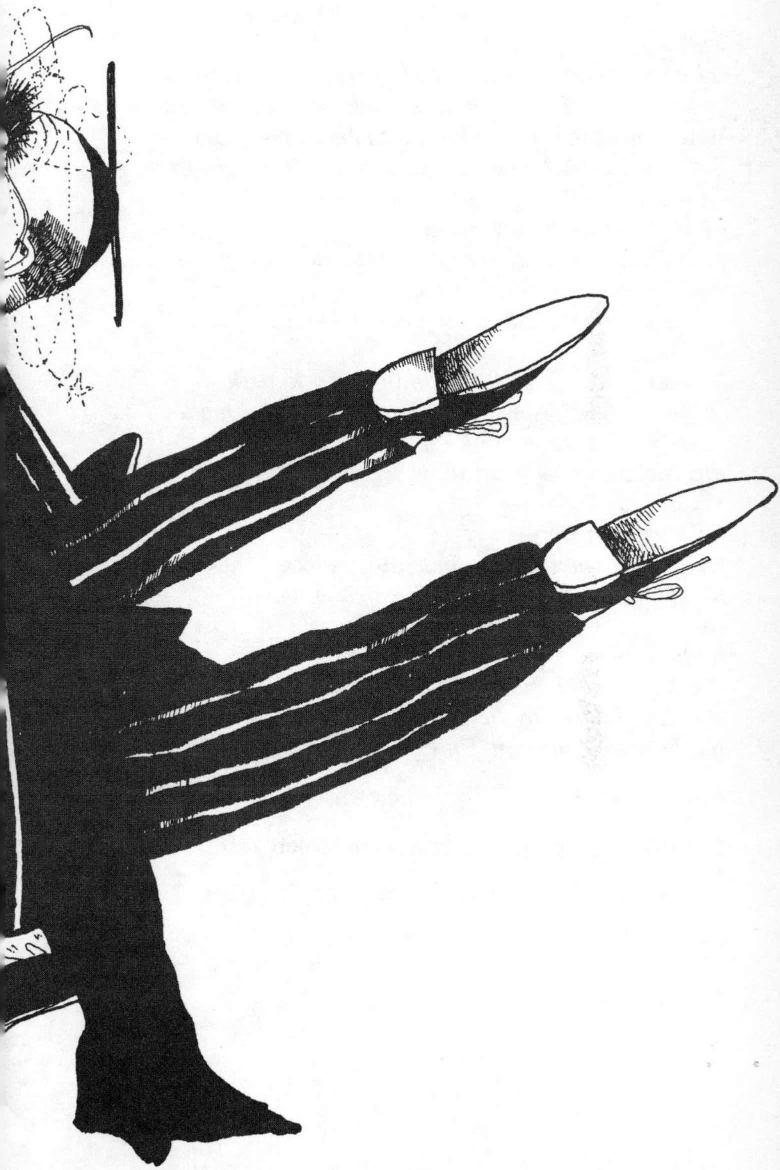

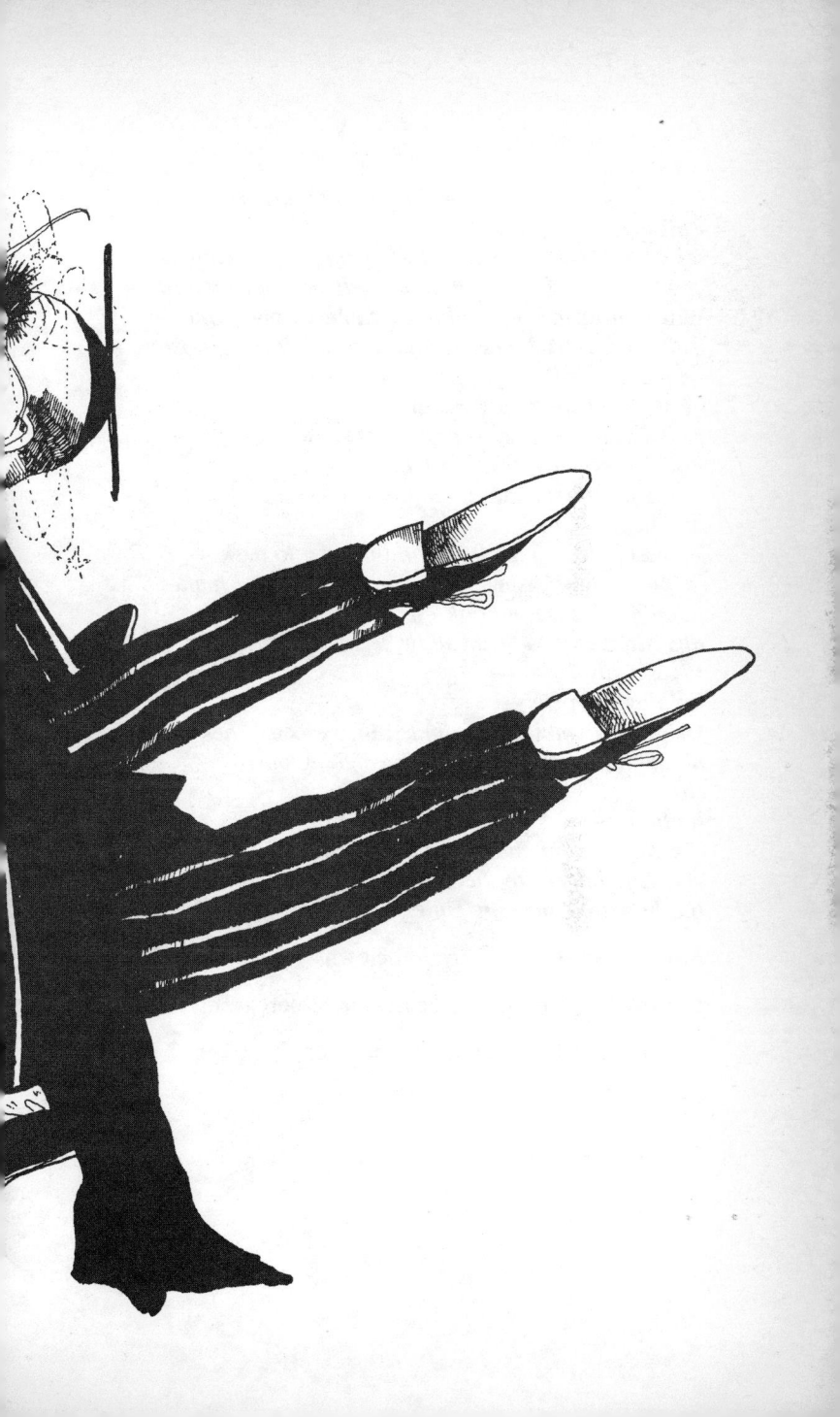

falls backwards —
catch him —
Molereasons *falls forwards into* **Puff**'s *arms —*
Puff *carts him to desk —*
Puff *puts* **Molereasons** *at desk facing wrong way —*
as soon as **Puff** *leaves him he nods into blackboard —*
Puff *returns to desk and turns* **Molereasons** *front —*
Puff *models* **Molereasons** *into typical teaching posture —*
he makes his finger point at class —
he sticks his finger up his nose —
he twists **Molereasons**' *mouth into a scowl —*
Puff *sits down with other* **Clowns** *—*
they wait for something to happen —
nothing does —
Weasel *picks up the book and takes it to desk —*
he pulls **Molereasons**' *finger out of nose and makes it point at passage in book —*
tilts **Molereasons**' *head so he seems to be reading —*
Weasel *sits down —*
nothing happens —
Drippens *comes up and puts* **Molereasons**' *stick in his hand and models him into threatening pose —*
sits —
nothing —
Pimple *goes up and blows in his ear —*
and Life returns to the Professor —
but he's gone back in Time.

Molereasons Good morning, clowns.

Clowns Good morning, Professor Molereasons!

Molereasons Chapter thirty-one.

Clowns Chapter thirty-FOUR.

Bell sounds.

Puff Breaktime, Sir!

Molereasons Breaktime! But we've only been here a minute!

But the **Clowns** *charge out to the playground.*

What's happening? I must get a grip of myself.

Molereasons *scratches his head —
he exits through Double Doors C.*

Interval

Act Two

Re-enter **Clowns** *noisily —*
Re-enter **Molereasons** *sneakily —*
as **Clowns** *become aware of* **Molereasons** *they quieten down, and take their places.*

Molereasons Chapter thirty-four.

Clowns Chapter thirty-four.

Molereasons (*reading*) 'The dying idiot. An old idiot lies on the point of death. He calls his three sons to his bedside and addresses them thus: "Whichever one of you can make me laugh the most to him will I leave everything." ' Puff is the dying idiot. You others are the three sons. Begin.

Puff *gets mattress out of the cupboard.*

A chance for you to really let yourself go in this one, class. In this one you're meant to be funny!

Molereasons *assists* **Puff** *into character and situation.*

'An old (**Puff** *does his old.*)
idiot (**Puff** *adds idiot.*)
lies (**Puff** *lies.*)
on the point (**Puff** *goes 'ouch' as if pricked in bum.*)
of death' (**Puff** *attempts to look poorly.*)

Puff (*in character of old idiot*) My sons, my sons, my time is almost comeblebum. Come into my bedroom, boys, that I may speak with 'ee.

Sons mime coming in through door one by one —
Weasel *is last —*

Act Two 41

he can't open imaginary door —
he breaks through imaginary wall to other side —
opens imaginary door from inside —
goes back out through imaginary hole in imaginary wall
and comes in through imaginary door.

Puff I want 'ee to make me laugh my last laugh and that right hoarsely. (**Weasel** *whinnies.*) So let's cut the cackle and jest get on with it. Jest get on with it! The son who makes me laugh the most shall have all my puds and chapels. Right, son the first, standing there in your pants, make me laugh.

Drippens *as son the first makes silly faces.*

I don't get it.

Pimple *as son the second makes silly faces at father.*

I don't get it.

Weasel *does funny faces and silly walks.*

I don't get it.

The Old Idiot suddenly notices **Professor Molereasons.**

O yes! Now that's what I calls funny!

Puff *laughs hysterically at* **Molereasons'** *face —*
summons **Weasel** *to his side.*

Weasel Shhhh! Daddy wants to tell us something.

Pimple What's he saying?

Weasel (*reporting what* **Puff** *is whispering and snickering into his ear*) He says that him over there – the charming gentleman in the horn-rimmed spectacles – has won the funniest face competition and gets all Dad's got.

Pimple What all's he gonna get then?

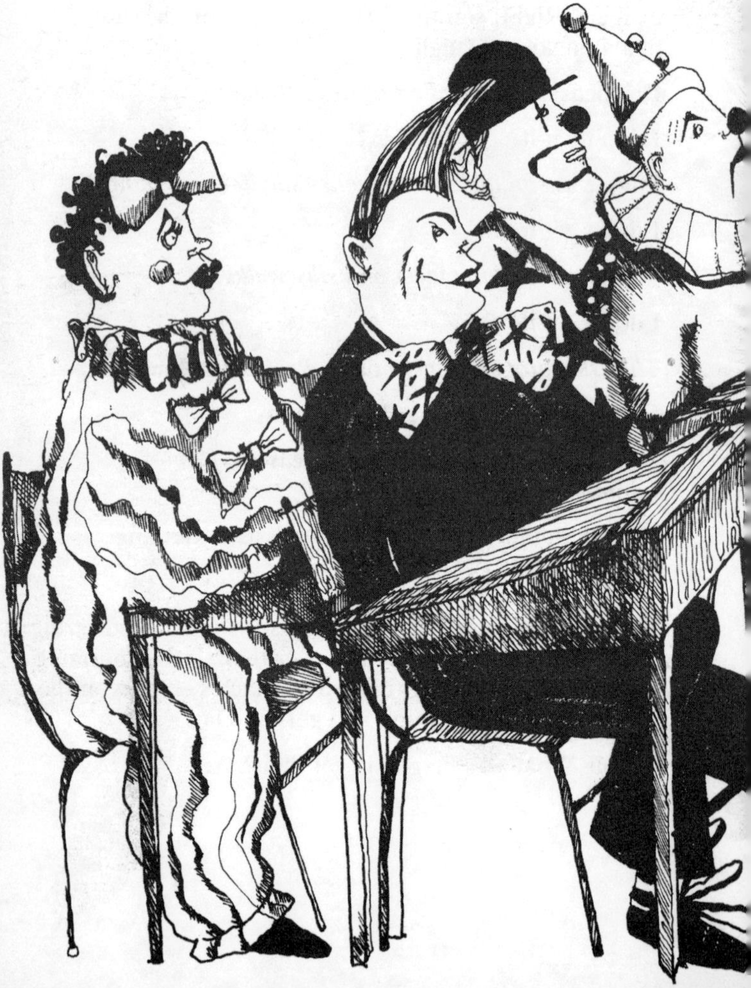

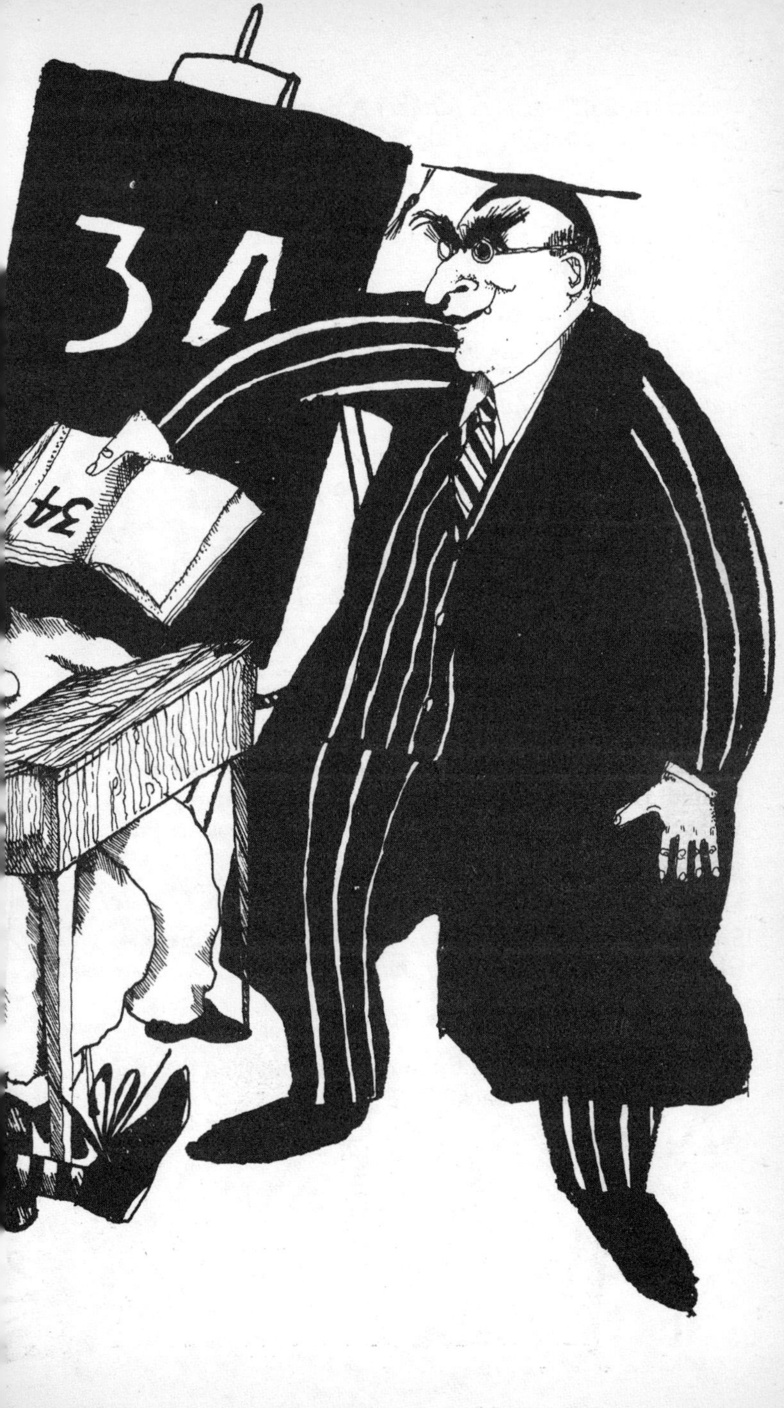
34

44 School for Clowns

Weasel (*as* **Puff** *whispers further*) A castle – he's going to get a castle – a knight's castle.

Drippens Oo, a knight's castle.

Puff Knight's Castle Soap – but it fell on the floor and got all hairs in it!

Old Idiot laughs himself to death —
dies with arms and legs sticking up in air —
Weasel *gives one leg a little flick —*
and stiff dead Idiot falls on his side.

Molereasons Well, that was beginning to border on impertinence . . . It's a good job I'm a sport.

Molereasons *laughs —*
laughs close-up into **Clowns**' *faces —*
Molereasons' *laughter becomes maniacal —*
Clowns *are frightened —*
they seek refuge under mattress —
pursued by laughing, demented **Molereasons**.

Molereasons You're all so funny, aren't you, you clowns! Drippens! (*Laughs and grossly impersonates* **Drippens**.) Pimple! (*Laughs and grossly impersonates* **Pimple**.) Weasel! (*Laughs and grossly impersonates* **Weasel**.) Puff!

Molereasons *goes to town on his* **Puff** *impersonation —*
Molereasons' *laughter turns to tears —*
Molereasons *exits Double Door C., weeping profusely —*
Clowns *creep out from under mattress.*

Pimple What a thing. Was he serious?

Puff It was a fit. Fits last three minutes and then that's it and they don't come back.

Weasel I hope you're right.

Act Two   45

Pimple I think we were a bit horrible to him. We definitely weren't lovely.

Puff Yes, but he's not lovely.

Pimple If we were lovely to him he would be lovely to us.

Drippens What do you have to do to be lovely?

Pimple This sort of thing. (*She pads up to* **Drippens** *and kisses him.*)

Weasel Pimple loves Drippens!

Puff (*to* **Drippens**) A Gent would return that kiss.

Drippens Really?

Weasel Do you want to break the heart of your beloved?

Drippens No.

Puff Well, get in there and kiss her.

Drippens (*shyly going over to* **Pimple**) No, not while you're looking.

Puff Obviously we shall look the other way while you actually do it.

Drippens Promise?

Weasel Yes, we'll look the other way. Promise.

Puff *and* **Weasel** *demonstrate looking the other way.*

Drippens You're peeping!

Weasel No we wasn't, was we?

Puff Nor we! (*Actually they were.*) We'll hide behind the cupboard. (*They get behind cupboard.*) Now go on and kiss her. You mustn't keep a Lady waiting.

46   School for Clowns

Drippens *kisses* **Pimple** —
Pimple *pads joyfully into audience to share her happiness with them.*

Puff *and* **Weasel** Drippens loves Pimple!

Drippens You did peep!

Drippens *slings open cupboard door, which bashes into faces of* **Puff** *and* **Weasel** —
they are trapped, dazed, behind cupboard door —
Drippens *comes out of cupboard with hand mirror* —
looks at his cheeks in mirror —
paints large lipstick lips on his cheek —
puts mirror back in cupboard —
shuts cupboard door —
stiff bodies of **Weasel** *and* **Puff** *crash to floor* —
Drippens *moons about* —
Weasel *comes to* —
sees **Pimple** *in audience* —
goes after her —
Puff *comes to and gives commentary in twit-language.*

Weasel Come back, Pimple. You know you mustn't be out there. (*Grabbing her and dragging her back.*) It's Sir you said you wanted to be lovely to.
Pimple I was practising being lovely.
Weasel Well, practise on Sir.

Pimple (*now back on stage*) The Practice of Love.

Drippens *moons in corner* —

Molereasons *enters Double Door C.* —
Weasel *and* **Puff** *dive to their places* —
Pimple *vamps towards* **Molereasons** —
she kisses him.

Molereasons Pimple! What on earth's the game, Woman!

Act Two 47

Pimple We weren't being lovely to you and now we want to be lovely to you.

Molereasons No! No! You mustn't! There mustn't be any of that, thank you!

Pimple What a THING. (*She sits down.*)

Molereasons (*regaining composure. Goes to desk. Opens book*) 'Chapter – ' where is Drippens?

Puff, **Weasel** *and* **Pimple** Chapter where is Drippens.

Molereasons No. No. Where is Drippens?

Weasel He's gone off.

Molereasons Gone off?

Puff (*miming dynamite explosion*) Gone off!

Weasel Gone off! (*Miming pong.*)

Molereasons Bah!

Puff Actually, Sir, he's in love.

Molereasons In love!

Drippens *dances out from corner —*
does Love Ballet —
dances to his place —
Molereasons *points at lipstick mark on* **Drippens**' *cheek.*

Molereasons Drippens, who gave you that? Speak out loud and fearlessly, lad.

Drippens I have found true love, Sir.

Molereasons Love is undoubtedly a many splendoured thing, Drippens – but beware you don't fool with it lest it fool with you.

48   School for Clowns

This last warning triggers off an old sorrow in
Molereasons' *memory —*
he forgets entirely where he is as he murmurs.

Molereasons Mabel!

Molereasons *kisses the lost Mabel of his mind —*
suddenly realises he is in a classroom of clowns and not
the boudoir of Mabel.

Molereasons Right, class, I think it will be the best thing for all of us if we put all our concentration into the reading of the next chapter.

He mops his brow.

Molereasons 'Chapter one hundred and three.'

Clowns Chapter one hundred and three.

Molereasons (*reading*) 'The Incredibly Wealthy Baron Grabbit requires a new servant. Three men are on the short list for the position. Baron Grabbit will choose the most humble, grovelling and toadying of the three.' Weasel is the first applicant. Pimple is the second applicant, and Drippens . . .

Pimple Is the third applicant.

Molereasons Thank you and Puff is the Baron. Begin.

Puff I am the Incredibly Wealthy Baron Grabbit in my pants. Come over here, worm! Go over there worm! Speak up! Be quiet! I can't hear you! Shut up! Bum! Bum-bum! Bogies!

Molereasons All right, thank you, Puff. I don't think you've quite got hold of the character of the Baron there. The Baron is an old time gentleman – he walks like an old time gentleman —

Act Two   49

Molereasons *hitches up his trousers and demonstrates calf-conscious Restoration-style walking —*
Puff *attempts it.*

– and he talks like an old time gentleman –

Molereasons *gives* **Puff** *his stick to aid his characterisation.*

Puff Please. Thank you. A drop more tea, mother?

Molereasons Yes, that's more the idea.

Molereasons *now addresses the three applicants.*

Molereasons Now the humble and grovelling applicants, apart from general toadying will of course have to master the art of flattery. Thus it will emerge that one of you is better than the others. Begin. First applicant, Weasel. Go on, out you go.

Molereasons *pushes* **Weasel** *out of Double Door C. —*
Weasel *knocks on door —*
Baron gives gentlemanly wave of stick, indicating 'come in' —
Weasel *squashes face against glass of Double Door —*
Weasel *knocks again.*

Puff (*roaring*) Well come in!

Weasel (*comes in. Speaking very quickly and physically mawling the Baron in his enthusiasm to be toadiest*) God bless you, good morning and good afternoon, Baron Grabbit Sir, so wonderful of you to say COME IN in such a delightfully baronial tone of voice, that noise of COME IN was music to my ears, and your feet if I may say so are perfume to my nose.

Puff (*as* **Baron**) Who are you and what do you want?

Weasel Who am I? I'm nothing, a nobody, a no one. I'm a sausage. A teeny weeny sausage. In fact I'm not even a sausage. I'm the skin of a sausage. I'm the skin of a skinless sausage. I'm just a bit of left-overs on somebody's plate.

Puff What do you want?

Weasel What do I want? I want a job as your grovelling servant, and I've come all this way, O go on, give us a job, Puffy . . .

Puff Not bad.

Weasel Not bad!

Weasel *jumps for joy into* **Puff**'s *arms and kisses him.*

Puff Get off! Get off! Just sit down over there until I've made my decision. Next.

Molereasons Next applicant – Pimple!

But **Pimple** *is sitting hand in hand with* **Drippens**, *dreaming into his eyes.*

Molereasons Pimple!

Pimple *goes to the door.*

Molereasons This is a classroom not a cinema!

Pimple *knocks on the inside of the door.*

Puff Come in!

Pimple *goes out. She knocks from outside.*

Puff Come in!

Pimple *comes in backwards —*
she turns front and traps her fingers in Doors.

Act Two 51

Pimple Yaaahhhhhhh (*Pain now turning into worship of the Baron.*) Oooooooooooo Mr Baboon Sir, I am dazzled by your beaming face, I want to be your humble and grovelly grovelly servant, you can do what you like with me, you can kick me. (*She picks up his leg and makes it kick her.*) O Mr Baboon, please give me the job –

Puff O please don't cry on my socks, Woman.

Pimple *rises and bows deeply —*
Puff measures the depth of bow with stick —
Drippens *takes note.*

Not bad. (*Referring to the measurement of bow depth as recorded on the stick.*)

Pimple O Mr Baboon.

Puff Yes, well you just sit down there dear, till I've seen the rest of the applicants. Next.

Molereasons Drippens!

Drippens (*goes straight up to Baron.* **Drippens**' *theory is that it's all down to bow-depth*) My name is Harold Humblebum and I would like to be your toadying and grovelling servant. Shall I grovel now?

Puff In your own time.

Drippens And you'll measure how low on the grovelling stick. How low.

Puff How low.

Weasel Hello! (*Waving.*)

Molereasons Shut up, Weasel!

52 School for Clowns

Drippens All right – here I go now. Grovelling and toadying. Are you ready with your stick?

Puff Yes.

Drippens *bows.* **Puff** *measures depth.*

Drippens How was I?

Puff Not as good as the last man.

Drippens *has another go.*

Puff No.

Drippens *grovels ludicrously low —
a hole opens up in the floor and* **Drippens** *falls down it.*

Puff That's my man! Definitely!

Weasel A toad in the hole!

Molereasons *peers down hole and then goes to Door C., to see if* **Mr Bogworth** *is anywhere about.*

Puff Well don't just sit there! Fish my servant out of the hole!

Applicants yank **Drippens** *out of hole —
he is unconscious —
they listen for his heart-beat.*

Weasel He's dead. He bowed so low he broke his neck!

Puff Dead! My servant dead!

Weasel (*grabbing* **Puff**'*s stick*) Let's be your servant then, Puffy.

Pimple No, me!

Weasel What sort of humble and grovelling servant do you think you're going to make, bum-face?

Act Two 53

Pimple More grumble and hovelling than you, pongy-drawers!

Pimple *and* **Weasel** *fight for* **Puff**'s *stick —*
Puff *holds on tight.*

Molereasons Pimple! Weasel!

Fight for stick pangs **Puff** *down hole.*

Molereasons Puff! O no.

Weasel Now look what you did.

Pimple You did it, you mean.

Weasel *is panged down hole.*

Molereasons Weasel!

Pimple *jumps down hole.* **Molereasons** *picks up stick.*

Molereasons O Lord in the sky help me to find the words to express myself at this outrage!

Drippens *is lying inert, feet towards hole —*
Molereasons *stands between* **Drippens**' *feet and hole —*
he is peering into the depths.

Molereasons Come out of that hole, you clowns.

Life returns to **Drippens** —
he stretches his legs knocking **Molereasons** *down hole —*
Molereasons *shouts up from hole.*

Molereasons Drippens, this is Professor Molereasons attempting to contact Drippens the clown from this hole!

Drippens Ooh there's a hole here!

Molereasons Drippens, pull me out.

Drippens Pull your what?

54 School for Clowns

Molereasons Out! Get hold of the stick! (**Molereasons'** *stick appears up through the hole.*)

Drippens Get hold of the what?

Molereasons The stick! (**Drippens** *gets hold of it.*) And whatever you do, Drippens, don't let go! (**Molereasons'** *red face appears up hole.*)

Drippens Don't what?

Molereasons Let go! (**Drippens** *lets go.*) Yahhhhhhh!

Molereasons *disappears back down hole.*)

Drippens Oo I dropped Professor Molereasons down the hole. Oo-er. Poor old Drippens. What am I going to do now? I'll get into trouble for that, won't I (*To audience.*) Where could I hide?

Wherever is suggested on stage **Drippens** *thinks of snags. Eventually he or the audience decide he should hide in the auditorium.*

Drippens You won't give me away, will you?

Weasel, **Puff**, **Pimple** and **Molereasons** *come up out of hole* —
Molereasons *is assisted by* **Weasel** *humping his rear and* **Puff** *heaving on stick.*

Molereasons Go on! Ah! Good. Now you clowns just keep well away from that hole until poor Mr Bogworth can get it mended. Where is Drippens?

Puff Somewhere else.

Weasel Gone to town.

Pimple A gone down town clown.

Puff And you've got a frown because he's a gone down town clown.

Pimple And you've got a brown frown because he's a gone down town clown in a white gown.

Weasel and you've got a brown frown because he's a gone down town clown in a white gown with his knickers hanging down!

Molereasons All right, that's quite enough thank you. Drippens, where are you? Drippens, if you don't come back here immediately your punishment will be too frightful to contemplate! Bah! Find Drippens!

Puff, **Pimple** *and* **Weasel** *charge in and out of the three doors, the cupboard and the hole in the wall, looking for* **Drippens** —
Molereasons *falls down hole* —
as he tries to get out the three **Clowns** *run over his head, without seeing him* —
Molereasons *heaves himself out of hole.*

Molereasons Drippens, when I find you I'm going to wallop you into next year!

Drippens (*from auditorium*) O no.

Molereasons Drippens, you're out there in the auditorium.

Drippens Yes!

Molereasons (*getting large torch out of the cupboard*) Have I lifted the ban on going into the auditorium?

Drippens Yes.

Molereasons (*scanning the audience with torch*) Have I

not rather taken great pains to stress the undesirability
of going into the audience . . . ?

Drippens Yes – no – yes.

Molereasons (*spotting* **Drippens**) Come back up here
immediately, you wretched clown.

Drippens (*two steps stagewards one step back*) No yes yes
no (*etc.*).

Molereasons Drippens, hurry up!

Unseen by **Molereasons** *the other three clowns go into the
audience.*

Molereasons Drippens, lad, do you hear that racket the
audience is making? They are indignant at your gross
behaviour! Your unpardonable behaviour is already
beginning to affect large pockets of the audience!
Drippens get a grip of yourself! Up you come, you
miserable, naughty, nasty little clown!

Drippens *is now onstage.*

What have you to say in your defence?

Drippens *howls.*

Don't howl – speak! Are you afraid?

Drippens Yes!

Molereasons I want the truth now, Drippens – you are
definitely frightened by me and my old-fashioned
teaching methods . . . ?

Drippens Yes.

Molereasons Well, that's good, Drippens. That is how it
ought to be. Authorities agree that fear and
concentration go hand in hand. I shall use you as an

example, Drippens, an example to the other three, but they're not here either!!! O this is too silly! I am unable to work under these conditions!

Molereasons *exits C., slamming door.*

Drippens (*happily*) Whoo – hoo Pimple!

Pimple (*from audience*) Whoo – hoo Little Dripper!

Molereasons (*barging back in*) Drippens, I'm holding you personally responsible to see to it that those other three clowns are back in here by the time I return. If they're not back here by the time I return your punishment will be frightful – I shall tear off your pom-poms! (*Exits C., slamming door.*)

Drippens You've got to come back here.

Weasel No, I'm going to stay with the kids.

Pimple We're being lovely with them.

Drippens But he's gonna tear off me pom-poms.

Puff Stick your pom-poms on his desk and get down here.

Drippens O please stop it. Please come back or I'm going to get into terrible trouble.

Pimple Come down here, Little Dripper!

Drippens It's all right for you down there having a good time, I mean I'm glad you're down there having a good time it's just that if I was down there having a good time I wouldn't be having a good time at all because I'd be thinking all the time of what terrible trouble little Drippens is going to get into when he gets back here.

Molereasons (*barging back in*) One more thing,

Drippens, the next chapter will be a test chapter and we know what that means, don't we?

Molereasons *chuckles maniacally —*
forgets to open Double Door and bashes into it —
sprawls —
his spectacles have come off —
wanders blindly about classroom tapping his way with stick.

Molereasons Can you see my spectacles anywhere, please, Drippens?

Drippens (*finds the spectacles. Wonders whether to give them back or not. Eventually he decides he will*) Here you are, Sir.

Molereasons Thank you.

Puts them on —
but still can't see —
discovers glass has come out of them —
rages.

Molereasons This unfortunate mishap has put me in an even worse mood for your test chapter! (*He fumbles his way to the door and exits.*)

Pimple What a thing – eh?

Puff *twitty-puffs.*

Weasel (*climbing back on stage followed by the other two*) So it's shitty old test time!

Pimple We've dung it now.

Drippens I'm frightened!

Pimple It's all right, Little Dripper – we'll get through it somehow.

Act Two   59

They form a tableau of irrational hope against unconquerable odds.

Puff But how?

Drippens Only a miragical could save us now.

Pimple (*an amazing idea has occurred to her*) What a thing! Yes. Yes. What a thing!

Weasel What? What?

Puff What?

Pimple (*referring to audience*) If they all come up here – they could help us with the test –

Puff We could paint them up as clowns!

Weasel Brilliant!

Puff Come on, up you come, clowns!!!

Clowns *apply clown make-up to audience's faces —* **Puff** *checks Double Door to make sure* **Molereasons** *isn't about.*

Puff Right, sit down, clowns – here he comes!

Molereasons (*enters, still almost blind. Taps his way to his desk*) Right, I want to speak to you four clowns very seriously. Do you know what you made me do? You got me in such a rage that you made me break my glasses, and I had to take them all the way up the road to the opticians, groping my way, lamp-post by lamp-post, making a complete spectacle of myself – quiet! – and the optician says he won't be able to mend them for a while, so I can't see you very well – but I think I can see you four wretched clowns well enough to give you your test chapter!

His nose is literally on the book, so close he has to be to the print to read it.

Molereasons And your test chapter is one of the very difficult chapters, 'Chapter fifteen.'

Clowns *and* **Children** Chapter fifteen!

Molereasons Curious! A multi-ventriloquial trick, eh? Made your voices sound like a crowd . . . Hmmm . . . well there we are, examination nerves provide us with miracles. Full concentration class on your test chapter – 'Chapter fifteen' –

Clowns *and* **Children** Chapter fifteen!

Molereasons The first time was funny! (*Reading*) 'The Wild Riders. The good people of the Westmorlands are in the grip of a sleeping sickness. It has sent them all stupid of head and dull of brain. Honest Arthur, Jumping Joe Soap and Moaning Mungo Wiggins go galloping through the Westmorlands trying to wake up the inhabitants.' Puff is honest Arthur, Weasel is Jumping Joe Soap. Pimple is Moaning Mungo Wiggins –

Pimple And Drippens is the Westmorlands!

Molereasons Idiot interruptions are not going to help you pass your examination. Let us just consider this chapter for a moment. I think the point at issue here is the immensity of area of the Westmorlands, which is to say that if you don't make enough noise the good people of the Westmorlands are going to remain stupid of head and dull of brain and you'll all fail your examination and we know what that means don't we! All right – off you go, Wild Riders! Begin!

Everyone Wake up! (*Etc.*)

An incredible racket —
Molereasons *is happy.*

Molereasons Thank you. That was good. It was more than good – it was excellent! You've never been as good as that in a test chapter before. I shall have to give you all ten out of ten. Four ten out of tens. I shall re-instate the box of sticky gold stars. I see this as a great triumph for old-fashioned teaching techniques – and an example to slack modern methods.

Mr Bogworth *fights his way to the Professor.*

Bogworth Professor! Professor!

Molereasons Who's that? Mr Bogworth, is it? Yes, Mr Bogworth, what can we do for you?

Bogworth The optician's finished your glasses, Professor.

Molereasons Well that is excellent!

Bogworth *puts the glasses into the hand of the almost blind* **Molereasons**.

Molereasons The glasses finished and class is finished!

Molereasons *puts specs on and sees painted audience – takes off specs.*

Molereasons I say, Mr Bogworth, I think the glass is dirty . . .

Bogworth No, it's not dirty, Professor.

Molereasons (*putting them on again*) Has the wretched man put trick multiplying glass in?

Bogworth No, he's put perfectly ordinary glasses glass in your glasses, Professor.

Molereasons (*goes and inspects painted audience. Finally* *his conclusion*) I'd like you four clowns to pay attention to what I've got to say to you. Wherever I look all I can see is nasty little Westmorlanders. I think the only deduction we can make is that I am batty . . . certainly off my conk to a degree . . . I think I shall definitely call class over for today . . . (*As he shuffles off.*) . . . I think what I shall do is go home, put my slippers on, and have a cup of tea . . .

The curtain falls.

Clowns on a School Outing

A Play by Ken Campbell
Based on the characters created by F K Waechter

'We all live slapstick lives, under an inexplicable sentence of death.' *Martin Gardner*

Clowns on a School Outing was first performed in English at the Coliseum, Oldham in September 1986, with the following cast:

Weasel	Stuart Golland
Puff	Clive Duncan
Pimple	Julia Ford
Drippens	Jeffrey Longmore
Professor Molereasons	Barry McGinn

Directed by John Retallach

The scene throughout is a beach.

Ausflug mit Clowns was first performed in German at the Schauspielhaus Bochum on 16 October 1985.

The four clowns were played by Hansa Czypionka, Evelyn Faber, Franz Xaver Zach and Ulrich Gebauer. Wolfgang Feige played the Professor.

The play was directed by Ken Campbell, designed by Anette Schulz with music by Willi Kellers.

Beach —
Rocks with rock pool —
Dunes and bit of countryside —
Wasp nest —
Five changing cubicles.

Sounds of sea —
Cries of seagulls —
Wasps buzzing round nest.

Noise of old car —
Wasps disappear into nest as cast enters in clown car.

Professor Molereasons *is driving car —*
he wears old fashioned driving goggles and mortar board —
seated immediately behind **Molereasons** *are clowns* **Weasel** *and* **Puff** *—*
in bucket seat at back are clowns **Drippens** *and* **Pimple** *—*
Pimple *is a lady clown —*
other three are gentleman clowns.

Car sputters to halt —
bangs and pops —
Molereasons *gets out and investigates engine —*
clouds of steam —
water and filth spurt out —
Molereasons *gets black face —*
Clowns *sing 'Mammy'.*

Molereasons Quiet! Shut up!

Molereasons *kicks car and doors fall off.*

Molereasons A fine start to the School Outing! I shall have to go and ring a garage. When I return, Weasel, my deck chair will be erected.

Weasel Yes, Sir.

Puff Is this where we're going then, Sir?

Molereasons It is not where we were going, Puff, but it is where we've come.

Drippens (*dubiously, pointing off*) What's that huge wobbly wet blue thing, Sir?

Molereasons Where?

Drippens There!

Molereasons (*putting on his 'distance' glasses*) The huge wobbly wet blue thing, Drippens, is the sea.

Pimple The Sea!!

Clowns The Sea!! The Sea!!!

Clowns *pour out of the car —*
caper in ecstasy —
Molereasons *takes off mortar board the easier to pursue them.*

Molereasons Clowns! Stop this! Stop this this instant!!

The clowns halt ecstatic reaction to mighty ocean.

Molereasons I'd like to make one thing clear, if I may, Clowns – I intend this to be an harmonious day; and while I hope you derive some enjoyment from this experience it is primarily intended as an Educational Trip. Harken to my words unless you'd prefer War!

Weasel War?

Puff War!!

Clowns War!!!

Clowns *launch into impromptu rendition of two world wars and more, particularly featuring sea battles, and landings.*

Molereasons This is intolerable!

But **Clowns** *are unstoppable —
resigned,* **Molereasons** *sits on running board of car —
running board falls off car with him on it.*

Clowns (*singing*)
You make fast
I make fast
Make fast the dinghy
Make fast the dinghy
Make fast the dinghy
You make fast
I make fast
Make fast the dinghy
Make fast the dinghy pontoon
For we're marching on to Laffin's plain
To Laffin's plain
To Laffin's plain
For we're marching on to Laffin's plain
Where they don't know a sheet from sugar paper, sugar paper, marmalade or jam.
I saw a silly boy
Sitting by the fire
I saw a Colonel
Rolling a tyre
Ee-i-oh
The dinghy's going
Ee-i-oh

68 Clowns on a School Outing

The dinghy's gone
Hold him down that Zulu-Warrior
Hold him down till I get there
Ah – ah – ah – ah – ah – ah

With fingers in mouths

Walla – walla – walla –

Molereasons All right, thank you clowns, now –

But they haven't finished.

Clowns
Calling A
Calling B
Calling all the Company
Calling A
Calling B
Calling all the Company
Lah dee dah dee dah dee dah dee dah
The Boers have gotten my Daddy
My Soldier Dad
I don't want to hear my Mammy cry
I don't want to hear my sister sigh
I'm going on a big ship
Across the Ocean Main
I'm going to fight the Boers I am
And bring my Daddy home again
Calling A
Calling B
Calling all the Company
Calling A –

Molereasons All right! Thank you! This is enough!! Quite enough!!! (*Having achieved order in the ranks.*) More than enough! All clowns back in the car! This instant!!!

Clowns on a School Outing 69

Clowns *get back in car.*

Molereasons I hope I won't have to say this again: this is an Official School Outing. Not the Silliness Olympics. Strict discipline will be observed at all times. You are in a Public Place and this means you are representatives of the School. The sternest of chastisements will follow close on the heels of any delinquent behaviour.

Seagull mucks on **Molereason***'s head —*
Clowns *laugh.*

Molereasons Quiet! What's the matter with you people? I was unaware that I had uttered anything the least bit risible!

Puff A seagull has just gone to the toilet on your head, Sir!

More laughter —
Molereasons *wipes head with hanky.*

Molereasons Thank you. Quiet! Now I'm going to have to trust you while I'm away phoning the garage. Puff!

Puff Sir?

Molereasons Sit still. Do nothing.

Puff Sir.

Molereasons Drippens!

Drippens Yes, Sir?

Molereasons Ditto.

Drippens Yes, Sir.

Molereasons Pimple!

Pimple Yes, Mr Molereasons?

Molereasons Likewise!

Pimple Yes, Mr Molereasons.

Molereasons Weasel!

Weasel The same.

Molereasons No. Put up my deck-chair.

Weasel Yes, Sir.

Molereasons Let us hope I won't be long.

Exit **Molereasons** —

Weasel *gets out of car —
pulls out* **Molereasons'** *deck-chair —
others watch as he spends spectacularly long time failing to erect it.*

Puff I think it's been made wrong.

Weasel What do you mean?

Puff *gets out of car —
disassembles deck-chair into its component wood and canvas.*

Drippens *and* **Pimple** Ummmm!

Drippens You were told to sit still and do nothing!

Puff (*referring to an invisible man*) Drippens, your friend has come to see you.

Drippens Where?

Puff Here.

Drippens I can't see anyone.

Puff That's because he's invisible. Isn't he Weasel? (*Winks at* **Weasel**.)

Clowns on a School Outing 71

Weasel Yes. He's an invisible man. That's why you can't see him.

They fool about pretending there's an invisible man there.

Drippens There's no one there at all.

Puff Yes there is.

Further manifestation of invisible man.

Weasel There certainly is.

Another manifestation.

Drippens No there isn't.

Puff Yes there is and his name is Tony Chestnut.

Drippens Tony Chestnut!

Puff Tony Chestnut.

Drippens Anyway I don't know anyone called Tony Chestnut.

Puff Yes you do.

Weasel O you do!

Puff Tony Chestnut wants you to come and say hello to him.

Drippens No.

Puff O please.

Weasel Please.

Puff Please!

Weasel Please!!

They grovel and out-grovel each other to persuade reluctant **Drippens** *out of car —*

72 Clowns on a School Outing

at last he gets out of car and comes to where invisible Tony Chestnut is supposed to be.

Drippens Where's this Tony Chestnut then?

Puff Toe! (*He stamps on* **Drippens'** *toe.*)

Drippens Ow!

Weasel Knee! (*He kicks* **Drippens'** *knee.*)

Drippens Yarch!

Puff Chest! (*He thumps* **Drippens'** *chest.*)

Puff *and* **Weasel** Nut!! (*They bonk* **Drippens** *on the head.*)

Puff Toe, Knee, Chest, Nut! (*Impersonating* **Molereasons**.) And when I want your comments, Drippens, I shall ask for them!

Drippens *cries, water squirting from his eyes.*

Pimple You've made him cry now. Cheer up little Dripper!

Drippens *continues to cry —*
Pimple *gets out of car to comfort him.*

Pimple I know. Have one of your sandwiches.

She gets **Drippens'** *sandwich pack out of car and unwraps it for him.*

Pimple Here you are, Dripper, a nice jam sandwich for you.

Gives him jam sandwich —
his floods of tears make sandwich soggy.

Drippens (*having nearly got over his tears, and then restarting as he sees sandwich is soggy*) My sandwich is all

Clowns on a School Outing 73

soggy now. And my Mum made it for me, really, really nicely and now it's all soggy! (*Tears*.)

Weasel You'll have to eat it with a spoon then.

Pimple *gets him spoon to eat his sandwich —*
Drippens' *sobs turn to sniffles and he sits down on ground to eat his sandwich with spoon —*
Pimple *sits beside him.*

Weasel *and* **Puff** *reassemble component parts of deckchair into fantastic thing.*

Wasps buzz up from nest —
wasp buzzes round **Drippens'** *sandwich.*

Drippens A wasp! Help!

Runs about frantically —
re-enter **Molereasons**.

Molereasons What is going on? Drippens control yourself!

Drippens It's a wasp, Sir!!

Molereasons *gets shrimping net out of car and catches wasp.*

Molereasons I have caught the beast! You may calm down, Drippens. A wasp is one of God's creatures. If we are calm they never sting. They only attack the hysterical. They are God's way of saying 'Calm down.' I shall release the little animal over here. Well out of the way. Off you go, little fellow.

It drops to the floor.

Puff It's dead.

Weasel You've killed it, Sir.

Drippens One of God's little creatures and you've killed it! (*Cries.*)

Molereasons Drippens control yourself, man! It's not dead! It's just having a little sleep. This is the time when wasps sleep.

Weasel It's not even lunchtime, Sir!

Molereasons The Spanish always sleep after lunch and wasps always have a little nap before it.

Drippens *is consoled but suspicious.*

Molereasons (*into the attack*) And would I be correct in supposing that in its recent history this monstrosity was my deck-chair?

Weasel Yes, Sir.

Puff No, Sir.

Molereasons Three bags full, Sir! And has a naughty clown called Puff, distinctly told to stay in the car – to remain inCARcerated, so to speak – got out, and re-assembled Sir's deck-chair into this decadent and loathsome example of Modern Art?

Puff (*proudly*) Yes, Sir.

Molereasons Get back in the car, Puff!

Puff Yes, Sir.

Puff *gets back in car.*

Molereasons Get back in the car all of you!

Other **Clowns** *get back in car.*

Molereasons Right. Everyone out of the car!

They get out.

Clowns on a School Outing 75

Molereasons Line up! Straight line! Tallest on the right shortest on the left!

They line up.

Molereasons I am so disgusted by this Class's behaviour so far on this outing that if I had my way I would take you straight back to school –

Clowns O, Sir!

Molereasons Yes! I would! But the garage, in that lax way which has become the appalling badge of our times, are unable to tell me when they will get over here to fix the car. So therefore, by Act of God, we are here. But since it is an Act of God, then it is clear how we should approach our time here. This is God-given time here now, so let us think for a moment how we should approach it.

Clowns *think —*
Their thinking erupts into routine involving angels, priests, bishops, etc.

Molereasons No, this is not what I meant! Cease! Be still!

Eventually **Clowns** *cease their God routine.*

Molereasons Well since you all appear to have a super-abundance of energy, I think the time is ripe for hard physical exercise. Weasel! You will lead strenuous physical jerks. Meanwhile, my deck-chair now having joined the worst excesses of Piccasso, I shall sit on this convenient mound (*wasp nest.*) and study my notes for the Nature Project. Weasel! Jerks!!

Molereasons *gets his mighty nature project book out of car and sits on wasp nest to study it —*

76   Clowns on a School Outing

Weasel *leads physical exercises —*
Clowns *get tired —*
they realise **Molereasons** *is not watching all the time so only exercise (frantically) when he looks up from book, and not at all when he is reading —*
becomes game in which **Molereasons** *tries to catch them slacking —*
eventually, he does.

Molereasons Do you take me for an idiot?

Puff *and* **Weasel** Yes, Sir!

Pimple *and* **Drippens** No, Sir!

Molereasons Three bags full, Sir!! This I had planned as a happy day, but some clowns sadly insist that it must all end in tears.

Pimple *and* **Drippens** Ummmmm!

Molereasons Thank you. I shall lead you in the Physical Jerks.

Molereasons *is still seated on wasp nest —*
Buzzing.

Molereasons Puff, is that you making that silly buzzing noise?

Puff No, Sir.

Molereasons Well stop it. Right. Jerks! Army style! Do everything that I do! Understood?

Clowns Yes, Sir!

But at that moment wasps sting his bottom.

Molereasons *races about in pain, clutching and waving at the seat of his pants —*

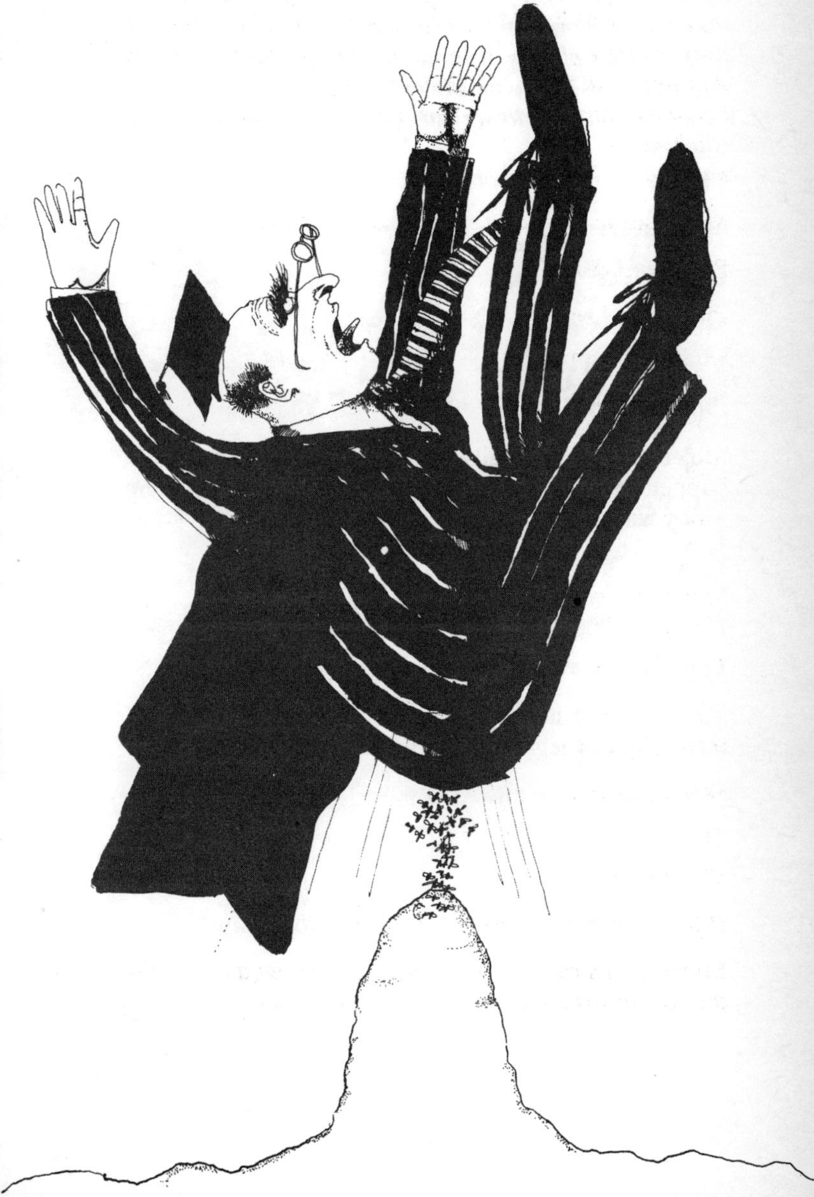

Clowns *do the same —*
as **Molereasons** *races about he tries to stop* **Clowns** *but they ape and impersonate his attempts to stop them —*
Molereasons *plonks his bottom in rock pool —*
Clowns *sit in pool with* **Molereasons** —
Molereasons *gets slowly out of pool with soaked bottom —*
Clowns *get out of pool.*

Molereasons Ridiculous! So now we're ALL wet!

Clowns Yes, Sir!

Molereasons And if we hang around in wet clothes – what will happen?

Pimple They'll get dry.

Molereasons Eventually, Pimple – yes. But what will happen to us? Anyone? (*No takers.*) We will get chaps, won't we.

Weasel 'Chaps', Sir?

Molereasons We run the risk of chaps on our legs.

Puff You mean RAF men will grab at us, Sir?

Molereasons Chaps! You fool, Puff! Sores! Sores will form! On our legs! Making walking difficult . . .

Clowns *do difficult walking.*

Molereasons Not to say, impossible!

Clowns *do 'impossible' walking —*
they appal themselves with the horror of 'chaps'.

Molereasons Exactly. We must get out of our wet things immediately. Into the huts and put on our swim things.

Clowns on a School Outing 79

They get their rolls of towel and costume out of car and go into the changing huts —
Drippens *finds himself in same hut as* **Pimple** *but this is spotted by* **Molereasons** *who hauls him out and into his own one —*
they wind up in changing huts in following order:
Hut one: **Molereasons** *—*
Hut two: **Weasel** *—*
Hut three: **Puff** *—*
Hut four: **Drippens** *—*
Hut five: **Pimple** *—*
Weasel *slams his door which makes* **Puff**'s *door open —*
Puff *slams his door which makes* **Weasel**'s *door open —*
Weasel *and* **Puff** *both slam doors at same time which makes* **Drippens**' *door open —*
Drippens *slams his door which makes* **Pimple**'s *door open —*
Pimple *is pulling dress over head so doesn't notice her door is open —*
Drippens *looks in at her as she tussles dress over head — he falls in love.*

Drippens I've got tingles.

Pimple *sees her door is open —*
and that **Drippens** *is peering and leering in — she squawks —*
Drippens *closes his door without slamming it —*
Pimple *slams her door which makes doors of* **Weasel**, **Puff** *and* **Drippens** *open —*
Pimple *opens her door —*
four **Clowns** *all slam doors at once which makes* **Molereasons**' *door fly open —*
Molereasons *hides his nakedness behind mortar board —*
Molereasons *slams his door and his whole beach hut falls*

over backwards —
Clowns *peer out of their huts at* **Molereasons'** *fallen hut.*

Pimple Ummm!

Drippens *turns round to look at* **Pimple**.

Pimple Do you think he's all right?

Drippens I've got tingles, Pimple.

Puff Are you all right, Sir?

Weasel Sir?

Drippens It's like butterflies in the tummy. In drizzle.

Puff Do you think he's dead?

Weasel Sir's dead!

Cry of ecstasy from **Puff** *and* **Weasel** *halted by 'lid' of fallen hut opening —*
Molereasons *emerges slowly —*
he is wearing old-fashioned swimming costume —
he assumes command.

Molereasons I want the names immediately of all those responsible for this outrage. Come on! Drippens, child, take that ridiculous expression off your face.

Drippens (*looking from* **Pimple** *to* **Molereasons**) I'm trying, Sir . . . but I've got tingles.

Molereasons You've what? He's what?

Puff *and* **Weasel** Drippens is in love, Sir!!

Molereasons Love! That's the last thing we want on a School Outing! Drippens, come out here!

Drippens *comes out in his old-fashioned bathing costume —*

Clowns on a School Outing   81

his legs are jelly —
soppy expression.

Molereasons Drippens I will not have Love raising its ugly head during school hours! Or after them! Or any time! Look at you! Stop it! Control yourself, man! What if War broke out and everyone was in this state?!? We'd be over-run by the enemy in minutes!! God in Heaven, boy, snap out of it! This instant!!

Puff *erupts out of his hut in his old-fashioned bathing costume —*
he has got balloons down his front which look like full and comely bosoms —
balloons are further inflatable by means of tube going to pump in lady's handbag which he carries —
he capers rudely, grotesquely, seductively.

Puff Love! Love!! (*etc*!!!)

Molereasons Puff cease this outrage immediately!

But **Puff** *has lost control and capers on.*

Molereasons Puff!

Puff *vamps suggestively round* **Molereasons** *pumping his bosoms.*

Puff Love! Love! (*Pumping.*) Love is in the air! (*Prancing.*)

Molereasons Stop this Puff! This is your last and final warning! This unseemly masquerade will cease this instant or severe chastisement will be the outcome! . . . Am I getting through to you, you wretched simple clown?

Weasel *and* **Pimple** *come out of huts in old-fashioned swimsuits.*

82 Clowns on a School Outing

Molereasons Right Puff! – I'm getting the stick. That's it! I'm getting the stick! (*Gets cane out of car*.) You, Puff, are in for the biggest wallopping of your undistinguished career.

Molereasons *comes towards* **Puff** *with his cane*.

Puff (*pumping up his bosoms further. Becoming an American gangster with lapses into cowboy*) Don't you come a step nearer, old timer! I've got nothing to win – nothing to lose – it's curtains – and that's the way I want it to be – I'm gonna go, and I don't care who I take with me – (*Continuing to pump bosoms*.) – yeah?

As bosoms become outrageously large, **Molereasons** *and other* **Clowns** *take cover behind huts, rocks and dunes.*

Molereasons (*the brave*) Puff stop pumping. (*Coming forward*.) Give me the pump, Puff.

Puff Get away old man. I've had it up to here with you.

Pimple Puff please! Please listen to reason!

Puff Reason? Yeah! Reason. But MOLEreason? Listen Pimple. I like you. I've always liked you. That time when I stuffed fudge down your knicks and you never squealed, remember? You're a good kid. But me? I've always been a wild one, Pimple. You. You? You settle down. Settle down with the pathetic Drippens. Raise a family of half-wits. I'm asking that. And I'm asking that you do it well. Do that for me, Pimple. (*Pumps on*.)

Molereasons Puff. This is your master speaking. Stop this insane pumping!

But **Puff** *keeps pumping —*
Puff *becomes frightened by size of bosoms.*

Puff OK. I might just be prepared to negotiate a truce.

Clowns on a School Outing 83

These are my terms – if you don't want yourselves and this beach blown into an ugly hole. You – (*To* **Molereasons**.) –

Molereasons Yes, Puff?

Puff Put your cane away and we'll all pretend this didn't happen.

Molereasons *reflects* —
Molereasons *looks doubtful* —
Puff *pumps some more.*

Pimple *and* **Weasel** Please, Sir!!

Molereasons *gives in* —
doesn't give in.

Molereasons No. No! No clown is going to hold discipline to ransome. Righteous judgement for your actions, Puff, there will have to be.

Puff All right. You asked for it.

Puff *detonates bosom* —
Puff *passes out, lying on the ground, dead.*

Weasel You've killed him, Sir.

Pimple You've really done it now.

Molereasons Puff! Puff! Breathe! Speak to me! (*Crouching at* **Puff**'s *side.*) He doesn't seem to be breathing.

Weasel Puff's puffed his last.

Molereasons Quiet. I shall have to administer the Kiss of Life.

Does so.

Drippens I thought you said there mustn't be any Love during School hours, Sir?

Molereasons This is the Kiss of Life. I am administering Artificial Respiration.

Pimple Kissing and Love are the same thing.

Molereasons Not in this instance.

Drippens If Puff's dead I'm going to tell my Mum.

Pimple There's a School Rule about killing pupils. Ummmmm!

Molereasons Quiet please! . . . and let me get on.

Gets back to Kiss of Life —
Drippens *and* **Pimple** *watching him, find themselves kissing each other.*

Molereasons He's coming round.

Puff *opens his eyes —*
he is horrified to find himself being kissed by **Molereasons**.

Puff Uggggh! What's your game?

Molereasons You had stopped breathing. I was giving you the Kiss of Life.

Puff Kiss of Death, more like!

Molereasons *about to answer, sees* **Drippens** *and* **Pimple**, *locked in an embrace.*

Molereasons Drippens! Get off Pimple!

Drippens (*explaining*) It's all right. It wasn't Love, Sir. I was giving her Artificial Insemination.

Molereasons *springs to his feet —*

Clowns on a School Outing   85

he thinks —
he parades, summons up his military background —
he pops —
he parades some more —
he sits down —
he becomes a philosopher.

Molereasons Drippens, this whole unseemly episode is clearly the result of Love. You allowed Love in where it had no right to be. What shall we do? And let us do the right thing. (*Tunes in.*) You are to sit right over here, Drippens. Sit over here, child. (*Taking him.*)

Drippens O, Sir!

Molereasons Yes. And well away from everybody. Hmmm. Weasel!

Weasel Sir?

Molereasons In the car there is a paper carrier bag.

Weasel Sir?

Molereasons Fetch me same.

Weasel Sir.

Weasel *gets paper carrier bag out of car —*
Molereasons *snatches it —*
Molereasons *puts paper bag over* **Drippens'** *head.*

Molereasons This bag, you will not remove, Drippens, until you can comport yourself in a seemly manner.

Drippens (*inside bag*) Yes, Sir.

Molereasons Puff!

Puff Yes, Sir?

Molereasons Puff, we shall set aside your appalling

86 Clowns on a School Outing

behaviour for the moment. It is possible . . . you have been punished enough.

Puff What, being kissed by you, you mean?

Weasel *laughs.*

Molereasons No. And you know I don't mean that. Weasel cease that cackling. (*He does.*) And take that smile off your face.

Weasel *raises his right hand and with it takes the smile off his face —*
but he keeps it in his hand!!

Molereasons We shall now get down to some hard work. I did have it in mind that a portion of our day would be devoted to some restrained fun, but that notion is now severely open to question.

Molereasons *opens nature project book —*
Weasel *puts smile back on his face —*
Molereasons *looks up.*

Molereasons Weasel!

Weasel *takes the smile off his face in the same way as before, still keeping it in his hand.*

Molereasons Throw it away. Throw it away entirely.

Weasel *throws his smile into sea —*

Pimple It's come up! Look! Weasel, your smile is unsinkable.

Puff Cor!

Molereasons Shut up! (*Reading from his project book.*) 'Wonders of the Seashore.'

Clowns Wonders of the Seashore.

Clowns on a School Outing 87

Molereasons (*reading*) 'The first, most of us experience of the seagull is – '

Seagull mucks on **Molereasons**' *head —*
the **Clowns** *nearly laugh but don't —*
Molereasons *seriously wipes seagull shit from his head with hanky —*
pause —
another pause —
Puff *nearly says something extremely momentous — doesn't —*
suddenly, **Clowns** *laugh hysterically.*

Molereasons Quiet! Control yourselves! Nothing funny! I think we'll skip seagulls and move on to the bee. (*Reading.*) 'The Queen Bee Lays Her Eggs'. Repeat please.

Clowns The Queen Bee Lays Her Eggs.

Molereasons (*reading*) 'The Queen Bee lays her eggs in an old mousehole. The eggs hatch into grubs. The grubs spin silky cocoons round themselves. Later the grubs come out of their cocoons as little bees. The Queen Bee gathers nectar from the flowers which she makes into honey for the young bees. All the baby bees are ladies. When they're old enough they will become Worker Bees and their job will be to gather more nectar to make more honey for more young bees which the Queen has produced.'

Pimple – The Queen Bee. Puff and Weasel – grubs which grow into young lady bees.

Drippens O, Sir, can't I be in it?

Molereasons Can you control yourself now Drippens?

Drippens Yes, Sir.

Molereasons Very well.

Drippens *removes his paper bag.*

Molereasons You can be a flower, Drippens.

Improvising with things from the car, beach, etc., they act out 'The Queen Bee Lays Her Eggs'.

Molereasons Good. Thank you. Very good flower, Drippens.

Drippens Thank you, Sir.

Molereasons And a nice stately Queen, Pimple. The grubs I thought were unnecessarily rude. Onward. (*Reads*) 'A Cuckoo Bee In The Nest'.

Clowns A Cuckoo Bee In The Nest.

Molereasons (*reads*) 'A Cuckoo Bee creeps in and hides in the nest. It stays hidden in the nest, stealing honey when the other bees aren't looking. After several days, the Cuckoo Bee smells the same as the other bees, so it can wander about the nest unnoticed. The Cuckoo Bee tries to kill the Queen so it can lay its own eggs in her cells. But two Worker Bees see the Cuckoo Bee about to attack the Queen and after a hard struggle they kill it.'

Pimple – The Queen again. Puff – the Cuckoo Bee. Weasel and Drippens – the two Worker Bees. Begin.

They act out the story of the Cuckoo Bee —
Puff *plays Cuckoo Bee as a loony —*
fight at end develops into dangerous free-for-all.

Molereasons All right! Thank you!! That's quite enough! The Cuckoo Bee is completely dead now, thank you! Weasel stop it! (*Reads*) 'The Queen Lays Her Last Eggs'.

Clowns on a School Outing   89

Clowns The Queen Lays Her Last Eggs.

Molereasons (*reading*) 'The Queen's last eggs are very special. Some hatch out into other Queen Bees. Others hatch out into Male Drone Bees. The Male Drones are very lazy. But one day the young Queens fly upwards and upwards and the Drones fly after them. Some Drones die in the air and fall to the ground, but the highest flyers of the Drones catch up with their Queen and mate with her so that she in her turn will be able to lay eggs.'

Pimple – A Young Queen Bee this time. Weasel, Puff and Drippens – Lazy Drones. Begin.

They act out 'The Queen Lays Her Last Eggs' —
when Young Queen flies **Drippens** *is determined to be 'highest flyer' —*
by nobbling other two he wins the Queen.

Drippens I'm the highest flyer. So I've got to mate with you.

Molereasons Very good. Thank you. Sit down everyone. Congratulations on being the highest flyer of the lazy male drones, Drippens.

Puff What is mating, Sir?

Weasel (*demonstrating*) It's putting a cloth cap on and being matey, isn't it, Sir.

Molereasons Er, not quite. It's the . . . necessary conjoining of two sexes towards the miracle of birth.

Drippens Is it . . . kissing?

Molereasons It's . . . similar.

90 Clowns on a School Outing

Drippens It's not fair. Why can bees and things mate and we can't.

Weasel Yes, Sir. Why don't human beings mate?

Molereasons (*pause*) Well actually . . . from time to time . . . every little once in a long while . . . they do.

Clowns Wow!!!!

Molereasons Now —

Weasel Have you ever mated, Sir?

Molereasons No. Well . . . I almost did once . . .

Weasel Gosh.

Pimple Pooo-eeee!

Molereasons Now —

Weasel Sir's gone red!

Pimple You're blushing, Sir.

Molereasons Quiet! Shut up! Settle down. Enough of bees. Onto birds . . . no we'll skip birds for today.

Puff Why was it you only 'almost' mated, Sir?

Molereasons Puff – enough.

Weasel He wasn't a high enough flyer.

A silence —
a halt —
Molereasons *is frozen —*
is it a coronary coming on? —
eventually he takes off his glasses and dabs his old eyes with hanky —
suddenly he lets out a strange noise, part sob, part sneeze, part bird warble.

Clowns on a School Outing 91

Molereasons Shall we all go for a swim?

Clowns Yes! Yes! Hoorayy!

They rush to car and get out rubber rings, water wings and armbands.

Molereasons 'The Water Code'.

Clowns The Water Code.

Molereasons Stay calm.

Clowns Stay calm.

Molereasons If you get into difficulties turn over and float on your back. Attract attention by waving ONE arm and shouting for help. If someone else is in difficulty in the water don't go in the water after him. Don't panic. Look for something to help pull him out – stick, rope or clothing. If you cannot reach him, throw any floating object – football, plastic bottle for him to hold onto, then fetch help. Understood?

Clowns Yes, Sir.

Molereasons I shall go in first and test the water for currents and tidal flow.

Molereasons *goes in sea —*
Clowns *watch.*

Pimple What's it like?

Weasel Watch out for crabs, Sir.

Drippens Is it cold?

Puff Can we come in now, Sir?

Pimple Is it safe for us, Sir?

92 Clowns on a School Outing

Molereasons (*off*) *does another strange noise – part sob, part sneeze, part bird warble.*

Pimple What's happened?

Weasel He's gone under.

Drippens Are you all right, Sir?

Puff P'raps he's gone down a hole.

Pimple He made that funny noise again and then just disappeared.

Weasel He's come up over there look!

Pimple Where?

Weasel There!

Pimple O yes.

Weasel Why's he got that funny look on his face?

Pimple Perhaps he swallowed your smile.

Drippens Why's he floating upside down?

Puff Because he's drowned. Dead. A goner.

Pimple We must save him. Poor Mr Molereasons. What did we have to do?

Weasel Throw things.

Puff That's right. You mustn't go in. You throw things.

They set to throwing all manner of things into sea.

Puff (*finally*) He's a goner.

Pimple He said if you were in difficulty you're meant to float on your back, so why's he floating on his front?

Puff 'Cos he's a goner.

Clowns on a School Outing 93

Pimple (*waving with both hands*) Help! Help!

Drippens No you're only meant to wave with one hand.

Clowns (*all waving with one hand*) Help! Help!

Weasel The sea's washed him up!

They drag the drowned **Molereasons** *out of sea and onto beach.*

Drippens What do we do now?

Pimple We'll have to give him the Kiss of Life.

Puff You can count me out of that game.

Pimple Well it'll have to be Weasel, me or Drippens does it.

Silence.

Ip dip sky blue
Who's it
Not you
Not because you're dirty
Not because you're clean
My Mum says
You're a little tiny bean.

This counts **Drippens** *out. She repeats the counting out poem with herself and* **Weasel**. *It counts her out this time.*

Pimple Weasel, it's you.

Puff Go on, son. There could be a medal in this.

Weasel *bends down to unsavoury task —
several times he nearly manages to get his lips to*
Molereasons' —
but eventually he has to admit defeat.

94 Clowns on a School Outing

Weasel I can't. I just can't.

Pimple O, out of the way.

She gives **Molereasons** *Kiss of Life.*

Molereasons *stirs.*

Weasel It's working! Keep going.

Drippens I think she's done enough now.

Molereasons (*coming to*) Mabel! It's Mabel isn't it?

Pimple *looks at the others.*

Puff He's got water on the brain.

Molereasons Hello Mabel!

Pimple What shall I do?

Weasel Pretend to be Mabel.

Pimple Yes it's Mabel, Mr Molereasons.

Molereasons Don't call me Mr Molereasons, Mabel. Call me Clarence.

Pimple Yes it's me, Mabel . . . Clarence.

Molereasons O my darling, I have longed for your return. Every night since you left I've tossed and turned scarce able to sleep with the aching and emptiness in my heart. And suddenly, I awaken to your dear kiss. O my darling Mabel, let me hold you in my arms.

Pimple *looks around —*
Weasel *and* **Puff** *encourage her to go along with it — they are enjoying it immensely —*
Drippens *moves in to try and stop it —*
he is restrained by **Puff** *and* **Weasel**, *who overpower him and sit on him.*

Clowns on a School Outing   95

Molereasons (**Pimple** *in his arms*.) O my honeybun, my darling heart, how I've dreamed of this moment. How I've dreaded it would never happen. I feel so light-headed. Let us skip and dance like we did in those golden days of childhood!

They skip and dance —
Puff *and* **Weasel** *laugh*.

Molereasons Who are these clowns?

Pimple I don't know, Clarence.

Molereasons (*to* **Puff** *and* **Weasel**) Is something bothering you gentlemen?

Weasel *and* **Puff** No.

Molereasons Well kindly mind your own business. O Mabel, just tell me – why did you leave me?

Pimple *looks round for help*.

Weasel Bad breath.

Puff Disgusting flannels.

Pimple Bad breath and disgusting flannels.

Molereasons Disgusting flannels?

Pimple Your mucky flannels.

Molereasons My cricket flannels?

Pimple Yes.

Puff No. His flannels in the bathroom.

Pimple Your flannels in the bathroom.

Molereasons My flannels in the bathroom? You mean my face cloths?

96   Clowns on a School Outing

Pimple Yes, they were so horrible they made me honk up.

Molereasons O Mabel – you should have said – I'll boil them – I'll throw them away – I'll buy new ones. My darling, may I kiss you?

Pimple No.

Drippens Don't let him!

Molereasons Just an itsy bitsy peck of a kiss, Mabel, that's all I ask for . . . my Princess . . . my Queen . . .

Pimple O all right, but make it quick and no slobbering.

Molereasons (**Pimple** *romantically in his arms, being drawn towards kiss*) I never thought this moment would ever happen, Mabel, especially when I heard you were dead.

He takes on his own words —
he remains frozen —
he looks about him —
he is out of his time warp —
he can't make out what he is doing with **Pimple** *in his arms.*

Weasel *and* **Puff** *laugh so heartily they fall off* **Drippens**.

Molereasons What on earth's your caper, Pimple! Get off me woman! This is an outrage!

He throws **Pimple** *off him —*
Drippens *steps up and slaps* **Molereasons'** *face —*
Drippens *picks up seaside spade and threatens* **Molereasons** *with it —*
Molereasons *defends himself with cane —*
A duel.

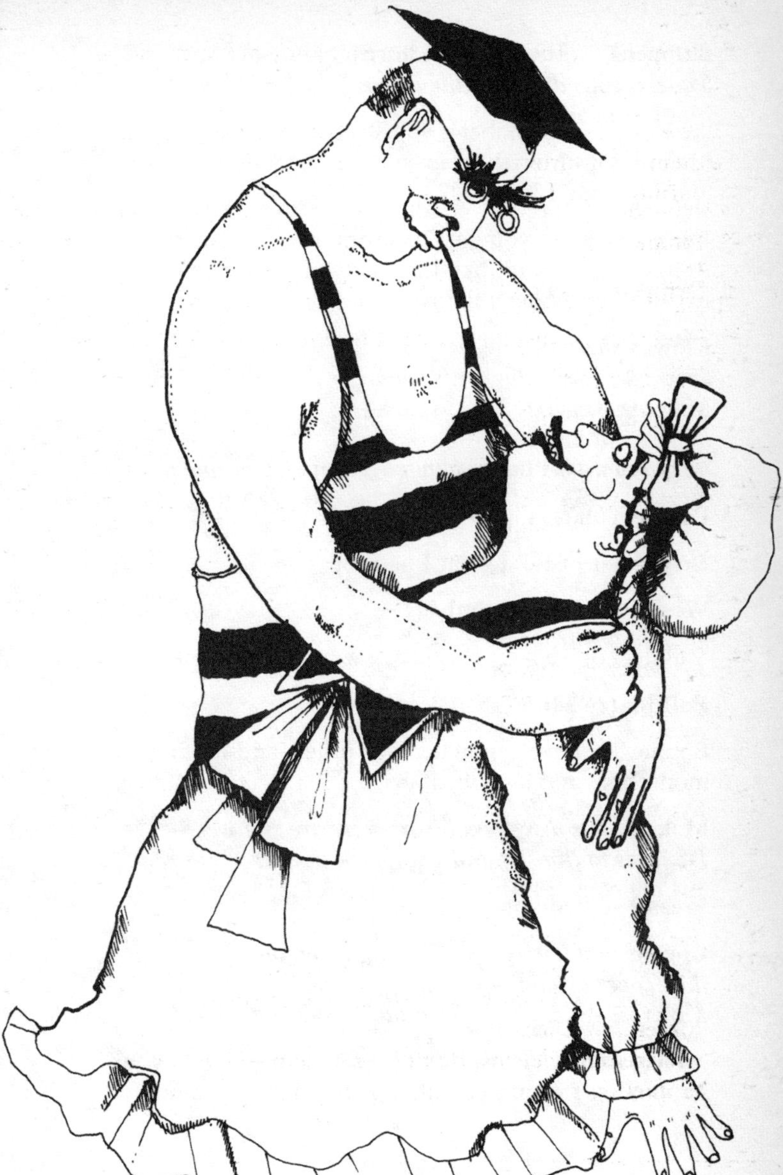

Drippens, *cheered on by* **Clowns**, *eventually has* **Molereasons** *down on the ground, his spade at his master's heart.*

Molereasons Mercy.

Drippens You're not worth messing up a nice spade for. I'm going to let you go. But from now on remember two things: one, I don't like the way you treat women and two, I'm watching you.

Clowns *cheer —*
Drippens *tosses down his spade —*
Molereasons *goes over to car —*
he gets out his towel —
he goes into his hut to change out of wet costume.

Pimple You're a hero, Drippens.

Drippens I just did what I had to.

Weasel You're a high flyer.

Pimple You've won me, if you want me, Drippens.

Puff Marry her.

Pimple Then we can mate each other, and I'll find a mousehole and lay lots of eggs.

Molereasons *discovers his trousers are still wet —*
He nods to himself and goes back in hut.

Weasel A wedding!

Clowns *perform clown wedding ceremony —*
they cheer as happy pair kiss —
Molereasons *emerges from hut in shirt and towel.*

Molereasons Clowns, don't let me interfere with your happiness. I would be failing in my duty if I didn't

Clowns on a School Outing

inform you that I've been a bit under the weather of late. Somewhat ill. Not very well. It may have made me behave . . . badly at times. I want to tell you that I'm sorry.

Puff That's all right. Just sit over there. And keep quiet.

Molereasons Over here?

But no one pays him any attention.

Weasel Hey, let's have our sandwiches now!

Clowns Yeah!!!!

*They go to car and get out their sandwich packs —
Clown picnic —*
Molereasons *goes to car —
sadly he sets himself up his fussy little bachelor table and stool, with table cloth, plate, knife and fork, mineral water —
he eats severely alone —
but with dignity —*
Clowns *continue comedy picnic.*

Weasel Pass me the pop.

Puff Pop!!

*They go into an Elvis Presley on the beach routine pretending that their spades are guitars —
They cheer themselves and throw their sandwich papers about.*

Molereasons (*his powers returning*) Now just a minute! This I will not have! At this I must speak! Litter! When we arrived this beach was unspoiled and beautiful and just look at it now! It must be tidied! Immediately!

Molereasons *and* **Clowns** *gather up litter —*

100   Clowns on a School Outing

*stuff it into litter bin —
but with such zeal, they burst litter bin and theirs and
loads of other people's litter bursts onto beach.*

Puff Great.

Weasel What do we do now then, Sir?

Molereasons *gets his picnic case out.*

Molereasons One thing is certain. It must not be left like this. We must think of those who come next.

Molereasons *leads* **Clowns** *in stuffing his case with litter — when he tries to close it, it bursts open at the hinges and litter bursts out again.*

Molereasons O no. My case is broken. And it was a special case. (*He sits down and cries, in sobs.*) And all this litter! And my picnic case!

Puff Means something special to you, does it, Sir, this case?

Molereasons *nods.*

Puff Something to do with . . . Mabel?

On hearing that name, **Molereasons** *rises, unable to speak. He makes to exit, a haunted man.*

Molereasons (*simply*) Please clear the mess up.

Exit **Molereasons.**

Puff Mabel gave it to him.

Pimple Or maybe he took her on a picnic and used it then.

Drippens Or maybe he'd bought the case to take her on a picnic and that's when she disappeared.

Clowns on a School Outing 101

Weasel She's dead now.

Pimple Poor Mr Molereasons! (*She cries.*)

Drippens *cries* —
Weasel *cries* —
Puff *holds out* —
but then he too cries.

They get themselves together —
they gather litter into pile.

Puff What shall we do with it?

Weasel *spies* **Molereasons'** *clothes drying over door of hut —*
he goes and gets them.

Weasel Stuff it into these!

Pimple Make a guy!

They stuff all the litter into **Molereasons'** *clothes —*
they make it look like **Molereasons** —
Molereasons *returns.*

Molereasons (*looking about the beach*) A nice clean beach. Thank you clowns.

Clowns That's all right, Sir, (Etc.)

Molereasons *picks up his case.*

Molereasons I'll get it mended.

Pimple I could help you mend it.

Drippens And me.

Molereasons I'll take it to a man I know. O no, he's dead. I'll find a man who can do it. But thank you.

102   Clowns on a School Outing

*He puts case carefully in car —
sees his stuffed clothes.*

Molereasons Good afternoon.

Weasel *works litter-stuffed dummy and ventriloquist's voice.*

Weasel (*Vent. voice*) Good afternoon.

Molereasons He looks familiar. (*To Dummy*.) Are you from the garage?

Weasel (*Vent. voice*) Yes. (*Dummy's hand falls off.*) Oops!

Molereasons Your hand's fallen off.

Weasel (*Vent. voice*) Yeah – it's one of them things when you get old, innit.

Molereasons But can you fix the car?

Weasel (*Vent. voice*) O yeah. (*Other hand falls off.*) Oops!

Molereasons You haven't got any hands at all!

Weasel (*Vent. voice*) No. Makes life – tricky.

Molereasons The garage have sent me a mechanic with no hands!

Weasel (*Vent. voice*) Yeah but I couldn't of done nuffink anyway – 'cos I don't know nuffink about cars.

Molereasons So that garage employs staff with no hands and no knowledge of cars!?

Weasel (*Vent. voice*) Yeah, but the good thing about all this is – I don't work for the garage.

Clowns on a School Outing 103

Molereasons You don't work for the garage, now! But you said you did!

Weasel (*Vent. voice*) O yeah.

Molereasons Why, in heaven's name?

Weasel (*Vent. voice*) Because – I'm a cantankerous old fart.

Puff Can I give you a hand? (*Puts hand back on Dummy.*)

Weasel (*Vent. voice*) O ta. Actually I'm the donkey man.

Molereasons (*enchanted*) You're the donkey man! Clowns, he's the donkey man. I'm going to buy you all a donkey ride.

Weasel (*Vent. voice*) Give us your money then. 10p a ride.

Molereasons 40p for the four clowns and have you got a very slow old donkey?

Weasel (*Vent. voice*) O yeah. I got a very slow old donkey.

Molereasons I'll have that one. Here's another 10p. It definitely doesn't go fast or prance or anything?

Weasel (*Vent. voice*) No. Definitely.

Molereasons Good. Clowns!

Weasel (*Vent. voice*) 'Cos it's dead.

Molereasons Dead!

Weasel (*Vent. voice*) Yeah – it got old – then grumpy – then very grumpy – then it died. Actually they're all dead. (*Dummy's head falls off.*) Oops. Me head's fallen off. I'm dead. I've died.

Weasel *emerges from behind Dummy and lays Dummy on beach.*

Weasel Donkey man's dead, Sir.

Molereasons He's not a great loss. I've had enough. Just leave him there. There'll be a beach man comes along later whose job it is to sort out corpses and things. Don't play with the body. Just leave it where it is. I'll leave my 50p with him to help with his funeral arrangements.

Weasel (*who has the 50p*) O that's really nice, Sir.

Molereasons Yes. He may have been quite a nice chap before he wound up a . . .

Puff Cantankerous old fart?

Molereasons I really just need a little nap. Free time now clowns. Don't do anything dangerous. Move that poor old man near me. He wouldn't have always been like that, you know. Wake me up if the real garage man comes. Build sandcastles and things.

Molereasons *falls asleep —*
Clowns *attempt sandcastle —*
they bury **Molereasons** *in sand so he's only a head —*
car starts itself up and starts to drive itself off —
Weasel *sees car.*

Weasel The car's going without us!

Clowns *pursue and jump into car as it drives itself offstage —*
just **Molereasons'** *head left on stage now —*
and Dummy —
Molereasons *wakes up.*

Molereasons What a lovely dream. I dreamt I met Mabel in Heaven. And she was looking so lovely. Clowns!

He looks around.

No one.

He looks down at his buried body.

I've got no body! I'm just a head! Aggghhhhh!!

*Realises what's happened —
to Dummy.*

Why didn't you stop them? Oh you're dead.

Getting out of sand —

You've got my clothes on!

Discovers it's his own clothes stuffed with litter.

You're me. And stuffed with rubbish. I hate you. I hate you!!

He fights and punches the Dummy with growing violence.

Molereasons *is really setting about the Dummy, oblivious to anything else —
then he ceases.*

Molereasons Clowns! Clowns! Where are you? The car's gone. Come back. Please come back. Clowns! This is hell.

Molereasons *wrestles and punches Dummy —
car comes back on with* **Weasel** *driving.*

Weasel Want a lift, Sir? We're off back to school!

Molereasons *looks up from his fight —*

car lurches off —
Molereasons *pursues it and is dragged off, hanging on the back.*

Blackout.

Peef

A Play by Ken Campbell
*Based on 'The Galoshes of Fortune' by Hans Andersen
and characters created by F K Waechter*

Peef was first performed (as *The Galoshes of Fortune*) by the Unicorn Theatre Company at Warwick Arts Centre, Coventry on 5 December 1991, with the following cast:

Weasel	Amanda Symons
Puff	Jason Yates
Pimple	Liz Brailsford
Drippens	Robert Neil Kingham
Professor Molereasons	Kieron Smith

The play was then performed by the Unicorn Theatre Company at the Arts Theatre, London on 15 February 1992, with the following cast:

Weasel	Cleo Sylvestre
Puff	Ray Emmet Brown
Pimple	Emma Gibbons
Drippens	Michael Webber
Professor Molereasons	Kieron Smith

Both productions were:

Directed by Richard Williams
Designed by David Collis
Lighting designed by Dave Horn

School room.

A Lady clown, **Pimple**, *comes in and sits waiting for a lesson —*
she looks at audience —
smiles —
makes faces —
makes friends —
begins an 'act' —
Weasel, *a clown with prominent teeth, comes in —*
Pimple *doesn't see him.*

Weasel (*impersonating their teacher,* **Molereasons**) Pimpole! – Sit down! Stand up! Shut up!

Pimple O it's Weasel!

Weasel *does balloon animals for the kids —*
Pimple *and* **Weasel** *and the audience get pally —*
Drippens, *another clown, comes in —*
he sees the palliness and gets jealous —
Drippens *goes into a paddy.*

Weasel Drippens is jealous. Do something, Pimple.

Pimple What shall I do, Weasel?

Enter **Puff**, *another clown —*
he looks grave —
so grave it silences **Drippens.**

Pimple What's the matter, Puff?

Pimple You look awfully worried, Puff.

Weasel Is your mother going to live?

Drippens Is it the end of the world? Have you lost your teddy?

Puff Worse. Worse than any of that. I heard them talking. There's going to be a Test.

Drippens O no, not a Test!

Weasel Grimmo!

Pimple Help!

The door opens —
Professor Molereasons *looks in —*
then he is talking to someone off.

Molereasons Ah. That's the new Spanker is it? Leave it out there for now. I'll have it wheeled in when I need it.

Pimple Get him in a good mood.

Molereasons Good Morning Clowns. Sit down. Stand up. Sit down. Yes, Sir.

Clowns No, Sir.

Molereasons Three bags full, Sir. (*Noting audience.*) How nice. You've brought a load of Homeless in off the streets. Somewhere warm for you to have a kip. You've left someone looking after your boxes have you? (*To* **Clowns**.) If there's any awake, tell them who I am and that I don't brook interrupting.

Clowns *tell audience that this is their teacher, Professor Molereasons, and he doesn't brook interrupting*.

Puff (*brightly to* **Molereasons**) Very nice tie you're wearing today, Sir.

Molereasons Thank you, Puff. Nice of you to say so. There's a shilling on the floor.

Puff *bends down to pick up non-existent coin —*
Molereasons *swipes his bottom with cane.*

Puff Yarrooo!

The **Clowns** *are now in place for a lesson.*

Molereasons Today is an Examination.

Drippens Please not an Examination, Mr Molereasons!

Molereasons Yes. The Big Test.

Weasel Not an Enid Blyton Test, Sir – didn't you kill all the third year when the results of their Noddy papers came through?

Molereasons No. This is exaggerated. I didn't kill all of them, no. Anyway, no, the Test won't be on Enid Blyton this year – this year's Big Test will be . . . on Hans Andersen.

Clowns *huddle in fear —*
then panic —
and riot.

Molereasons (*addressing* **Clowns** *through a loud-hailer*)
Complete calm by the count of three or I fire the cannon
. . . one – two – three!

And calm is restored.

Drippens O, Sir, not Hans Andersen, Sir, he makes you so unhappy.

Molereasons And that is why he's so good for you, Drippens –
A Hans Andersen hero falls in love –
and it's useless! –
She's a mermaid or a lady with her leg up her tu-tu –

but then at the very last moment, yes, these lovers are
united . . . *by burning together!* –
or being flushed down the pipes and into an insanitary
Scandinavian sewage system together –
uselessly they make it –
if there is to be a come-togethering it will be at a time of
no use –
in a place of no use –
but at that useless, awful moment, as we howl and cry
we *do see a pattern* –
and seeing the pattern:
makes it all the more awful!
You shy away from Hans Andersen, you Clowns,
because he's rough and tough and shines his torch into
dark places you'd prefer not to peek.
the Magic Galoshes.
The Galoshes of Fortune.
What are Galoshes?
What is a Galosh?

Pimple A Galosh is the little thing inside you that says
Heyup! I'd best jump out the window.

Molereasons No.

Weasel Is it the bits of crispiness in an old hanky?

Molereasons No.

Drippens Galosh is the feeling you get if you run not
very fast at a soft wall – it's like when you come upwards
under a cow on a Spring afternoon.

Molereasons No!

Drippens And the cow's name is Daisy.

Molereasons Shut up, Drippens – No!

Puff Something you wear?

Molereasons Yes.

Puff Would it be . . . a willy warmer?

Molereasons No!

Puff A willy cooler? – vital in Africa I would have thought.

Molereasons No doubt, but NO! – Galoshes are overshoes that you put over your shoes (*he is going into the cupboard to get these things as he speaks*.) to keep out the slush and snow and filth of the North – (*showing Galoshes*.) Galoshes – But Hans Andersen —

Clowns *cringe at mention of that name.*

Molereasons Hans Andersen wrote about Magic Galoshes. Galoshes of Fortune.

Puff What and you'd put these galosh things over your shoes and then Wheee-Heee anything you wanted?

Molereasons Yes. If you were lonely and sad enough, angels and fairies and wotnot would bring you these Galoshes of Fortune and you'd put them on and wish for what you wanted – go back in time to a happy time – loads of money – a change of wife – whatever – but this is the genius of Andersen – *when you got it you didn't want it* – in fact worse *it turns everything absolutely frightful!* Hee-hee!

Puff Magic Galoshes?

Molereasons Yes.

Puff And the genius of these Galosh things is that they don't just make things not better than they were, they make them worse – so who except the terminally thick would put these things on? (*Smelling them.*) – and they're smelly.

Molereasons Yes, yes. Just sit quiet while I look up the Answers. Not that I don't know the Answers. But it amuses me to see how they word them.

Molereasons is at his high desk —
looking up the answers in the back of his big book —
Weasel fastens a mirror onto a fishing rod —
extends the rod so that the mirror is looking over
Molereasons' shoulder at answers —
Molereasons looks up at Clowns —
sees his reflection in mirror —
sees he has a little spot —
squeezes it —
goes back to answers —
looks up at mirror —
sees rod.

Molereasons Clowns cheating, is it? Aha! An ideal opportunity to test out my New Spanker!

Molereasons goes out and wheels in the Spanker —
pulls off paper revealing the ghastly punishment machine.

Molereasons (*looking at his new toy*) The emotion I feel is very similar to Love.

He lines up and plugs in the Spanker.

Molereasons Get bent over Clowns and allow the Spanker to do his worst!

The Spanker grinds and sparks and wallops —
Weasel tosses a shoe into the works.

Weasel The Spanker's out of control!

Puff Sir! Sir! The Spanker!

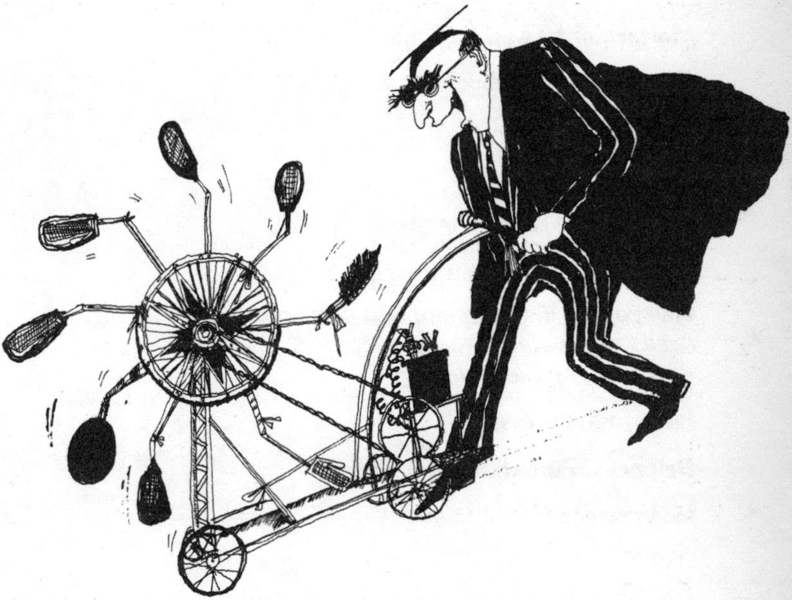

Molereasons *goes to investigate.*

Puff Watch out, Sir!

A spank arm elevates and swipes **Molereasons** *head — he hits the deck.*

Puff Too late.

Weasel Dead is he?

Molereasons Where am I? Oo stars! (*Counts stars.*)

Puff No, just brained.

Molereasons Twinkle twinkle little stars.

Pimple Quick – while he's got the sillies!

Drippens What?

Weasel What?

They huddle round **Pimple** —
she whispers the plan —
their faces indicate it's a great and naughty plan —
they go into the cupboard and come out dressed as angels, fairies and wotnot —
Puff *picks up the Galoshes.*

Puff (*to* **Molereasons**) Hello!

Drippens, **Pimple**, **Weasel** Hello!

Molereasons Who are you?

Puff We are Angels, Fairies and Wotnot.

Drippens Of the Magic Wellies.

Pimple We bring you the Galoshes of Fortune. With these on you can go back to a happy time or change your wife.

Molereasons I haven't got a wife.

Pimple Well that bit doesn't apply to you then. Go back to a happy time.

Molereasons A happy time? That's tricky.

Weasel (*referring to Galoshes*) These'll get you back there all right. They're Magic.

Pimple We don't even know how they work.

Drippens And we're angels.

Molereasons A happy time?

Drippens Just think of a happy time you once had.

Molereasons I'm not sure there ever actually has been one of those . . .

Pimple You must have been happy ONCE!?!?

Molereasons Yes I was, I think I was, yes I was happy once, yes, just for a moment, a long time ago . . .

Puff A very long time ago was it?

Molereasons Yes . . .

Weasel A very, very long time ago?

Molereasons Yes . . . when I was a young man . . .

Puff O a very, very, very long time ago.

Molereasons I was very poor . . . I'd come from the North seeking my fortune in Petersfield, in Petersfield, or 'Peef' . . .

Drippens 'Peef'!?

Molereasons Yes, the good people of Petersfield called it Peef . . .

Puff Is that because they were thick?

Molereasons No, it was just one of their charming little ways . . .

Pimple Anyway, so you were in Petersfield, in Petersfield, in Peef . . ?

Drippens And poor . . ?

Weasel A young man . . ?

Puff Not an old and crabby man . . .

Molereasons I was so poor I couldn't even afford braces . . .

Weasel Braces for your teeth?

Molereasons No. Braces for me trousers . . . I had to tie them up with a bit of frayed old knotty string . . .

Drippens It's ever so sad your one happy moment.

Molereasons I'd just got a job with the Butcher, I was the Butcher's boy, and I was slicing up the beef and then I saw this young lady going by . . . and . . . and . . .

Weasel What?

Puff What?

Molereasons She hadn't got any clothes on.

The **Clowns** *are shocked.*

Weasel What, nothing on at all?

Molereasons Just a frond . . .

Drippens What's a frond?

Molereasons Just a leaf . . . maybe a couple of leaves . . .

Pimple So what did you do?

Molereasons I waved a slice of beef at her and she smiled a smile at me and she had lovely teeth . . .

Weasel I expect her Mum and Dad had made her wear braces when she was at school. I'm meant to wear this (*a 'G' clamp*) but I find it too restricting.

Pimple Shhh! Go on.

Molereasons And I told her I was in love with her . . .

Big reaction from **Clowns**.

Pimple And what did she say?

Molereasons She slapped my face and said she couldn't even entertain the idea of going out with a boy who dressed so funny and raggedy . . . and I pretended it didn't matter to me (but it did) and I took a pinch of snuff . . . taking snuff was the thing in Petersfield, in Peef, in those days . . . it showed you were someone . . . and then Atchoo! I sneezed . . . and I sneezed my trousers off and then we heard this cough behind us and it was this Policeman so we ran up the road and into the *Duck and Diddle*, a charming little restaurant in Petersfield –

Drippens In Peef.

Molereasons In Peef, yes, and we said to the Manager of the restaurant, a dear man called Alec, that we needed a bath, and he said we could use his, that was quite all right, and showed us where it was, upstairs, and we got in the bath, and the water was lovely and warm, and that's when it was, that's when for a moment I was happy . . .

Pimple But what happened? Why was it only a moment?

Molereasons Then we heard the Policeman coming up the path, jangling handcuffs, and she said she had to go, and I said I wanted to marry her, but she was out of the window, all wet and gone . . .

Pimple And did you never see her again?

Molereasons Three months later when they let me out of prison (they let me out after only three months because I behaved so well), I asked all round Peef, but no, no one knew anything, and no, I never saw her again. Except in my dreams. And she was from the North too.

Drippens (*water squirting from his eyes*) Your happy moment is the saddest thing I ever heard!

Molereasons My heart was often to ask this question: Was there something more I could have done?

Weasel Well luckily we've got these Magic Galoshes.

Puff O yes, I'd forgotten, we are the Angels and Fairies and Wotnot who bring Galoshes of Fortune to poor, lonely miserable old farts like you.

Pimple And here they are.

Molereasons They really are real are they, these Galoshes of Fortune?

Weasel Yes.

Molereasons I thought they were just a story.

Pimple No, with these Galoshes you can have your chance over again.

Drippens You can go back in time with Magic Galoshes.

Pimple Put them on. (*She puts them on him.*) Now shut

your eyes and we're going to take you back in time to your happy moment. Are your eyes shut?

Molereasons It's very nice of you Angels to do this for me. (*His eyes tight shut.*)

Pimple (*helping him out of his trousers*) You had no trousers on if you remember.

Molereasons That's right.

Weasel You'd sneezed them off.

Puff *has got a tin bath out of the cupboard.*

Pimple (*to* **Weasel**) Help me get the rest of his clothes off.

Weasel (*finds the notion so repellent he can't do it*) I've gone silly in the fingers.

Puff *helps* **Molereasons** *out of his jacket and shirt — So he's now in his nasty long woolly underwear.*

Weasel Please no more! I couldn't live through the sight of any more!

They help **Molereasons** *into the bath —*
Pimple *undresses down to her clown underwear —*
Puff *is filling a bucket of water —*
Pimple *gets in the bath with* **Molereasons**.

Pimple We're now going back to your happy moment.

Molereasons But where's the water? I remember the water was ever so lovely and warm . . ?

Puff (*with bucket*) It may not have been quite as warm as you remember it.

Puff *pours icy water on* **Molereasons** *head.*

Molereasons Yarrrch! (*He returns to present time.*)
Where am I? What is the meaning of this outrage?
Pimple get out of this bath and put your clothes on! Why
am I in my underwear?

Weasel It came on ever so hot.

Puff And you became light-headed and just flung your
clothes off like you was in the ballet.

Weasel Often happens in the heat.

Molereasons (*dressing*) O and I've got a soaking wet
vest. And panties.

Weasel We tried to stop you.

Puff But there was no stopping you, Sir. It was like you
had the strength of twenty in your light-headedness –

Weasel Brung on by the heat –

Puff You had the strength of a whole Corpse de Ballet –

Molereasons What day is it today?

Drippens Yesterday.

Molereasons (*still a bit groggy, so taken in*) O, it's only
yesterday is it, well let me tell you what's going to
happen TOMORROW! Tomorrow is Test Day! There
will be no fun and laughter TOMORROW. Tomorrow
(*he happens to be looking at the calendar on the wall.*) – I
see from the calendar that it is in fact Today today! And
Today is Test Day. (*Swishing around with cane.*) I hope
for your sakes you do well. (*The swishings make him
aware of the dampness of his undergarments.*) This wet
underwear is a worry. I hope I don't get chaps.

Puff Chaps?

Weasel Chaps!

Clowns CHAPS!!!

Clowns *go into silly RAF chaps routine —*
Molereasons *blows his whistle on it.*

Molereasons 'Chaps' is a medical word meaning sores and possibly fungoid infected rubbings which distinguished older people might contract if their underwear is dampish. It has nothing to do with the regrettably silly behaviour sometimes to be encountered in Royal Air Force messes. And MESS makes me think of you. AND THE TEST. Hans Andersen. A man who in his life and work and art reminds us –

Puff *yawns hugely —*
Molereasons *glares at him, cane in hand.*

Puff I'm sorry, Sir, that's the noise I make when I'm really interested in something. All my family do it. A lot of people think it's odd. (*Yawns in a very interested, alert way.*) Please go on.

Molereasons – reminds us of the darker, doomier side of life. Is Life a Bowl of Cherries?

Drippens *enthusiastically holds his hand up.*

Molereasons Drippens?

Drippens Yes, Sir. (*See* **Molereasons**' *reaction.*) No, Sir.

Molereasons Three bags full, Sir! – Life is not just buns is it Drippens?

Drippens No, Sir.

Molereasons On occasion to be sure, a bun comes – but it's mainly waiting – as we prowl behind the bars of Life, hoping, wishing, praying to Lord God of All in the Sky, that soon will get thrown at us our next bun – we realise, don't we? – all of us – that this is what Life is – it's not BUNS – it is waiting and hoping for buns – and always the terror within us all – WE HAVE HAD OUR LAST BUN – THAT BUN YESTERDAY, LAST WEEK, MANY YEARS AGO – WAS THE LAST BUN WE WERE EVER TO HAVE!!

Puff Sir's crying!

Molereasons No, I'm not.

Puff Let me rephrase that: there is an issue of translucent liquid substance beneath one of your eyes.

Molereasons Is there? I think not. A trick of the light. Possibly rising damp from my underwear.

Pimple I think what you've got there, Sir, is a tear.

Drippens *starts squirting from his eyes.*

Molereasons Do you? STOP THAT DRIPPENS! Well I don't. (*Swishes cane.*) Test. Hans Andersen.

Clowns *groan.*

Molereasons Yes! And – the 'Galoshes of Fortune'. Remember – when you get the Galoshes of Fortune – you think things are going to go terrifically – but they don't, do they?

Drippens Yes, Sir, I mean, no, Sir –

Molereasons And I mean three bags full, Sir. – The Test is this, Clowns: I want a NEW story of the Magic Galoshes – which thinly treads the genius of Hans Andersen to walk the tight-rope between Loads o' Buns and No Buns Never Again No More. There was the Little Mermaid wasn't there? –

Drippens (*beginning to squirt*) O please, Sir! –

Molereasons Stop that, Drippens, who longed for the Prince, so had to not be able to speak and tread forever on knives – this is the stuff that educates you Clowns and tells you what Life is about – and the Red Dancing Shoes that keep on and keep on dancing and what do they have to do to the girl? –

Weasel Chop her feet off.

Molereasons Correct, well done.

Drippens *and* **Pimple** *weep together*.

Molereasons Stiffen the sinews, you sillier Clowns – we trudge and slop the marshes, with sudden deeps and quick-sands – quick-MUD! – he tested himself against the avalanche and the lacerating sandstorm – The Tin Soldier – Little toy tin soldier – only got one leg – falls in love with china ballerina – thinks she's only got one leg –

Puff But she had her leg up under her tu-tu, didn't she, Sir? He only thought she had one leg because he was thick.

Molereasons He was a tin soldier!! – and he falls out of the window and down a drain and is carried out to sea and eaten by a fish and the fish is bought by a cook who is the cook of where the boy whose toy soldier it was lives and she cuts up the fish and finds the Toy Soldier – or Tin Soldier and in fact it wouldn't be a TIN soldier – that was just their way of saying it in those days – it would have been of LEAD – and the Cook has found it and she's taken it up to the little boy's bedroom – the little boy whose lead soldier it was – and he says thank you, but when, well, AS she's closing the door he throws the lead tin soldier on the FIRE! – because he'd NEVER LOVED IT ANYWAY! – LEAD – let us see it melting on the coals – a meaningless existence – BUT THEN – the draught of the door closing makes the china ballerina fall in the fire –

Puff And that was that very ballerina that he thought was one-legged like himself, although, actually her leg was stuck up in her tu-tu – but he thought she only had one leg because he was thick – sorry, not thick – lead – or maybe because he went to an all-male school for leaden tin soldiers from where you'd come out just not knowing what all girls might get up to with their legs and tu-tus?

Molereasons The point is this: It's not all buns, Hans Andersen says, but maybe there's a pattern, a pattern beyond buns, which occasionally we glimpse – the ballerina and the tin soldier UNITED – BUT ONLY AS THEY BURN AWAY – does any Clown receive the poetry of this?

Puff I wouldn't fall for a one-legged ballerina anyway – because I have a Thing – there has to be the proper two legs for me – but now I think about it – a ONE-legged ballerina . . . (*Yawns hugely.*) Yes, wow, she's got my vote and please let me die on the coals with her! I love her! I love her!

Molereasons The TEST. The Galoshes of Fortune. And I want a new story. And I'd like it in rhyme, please. And no vulgarity. Gentlemen and Lady I give you one minute . . .

The **Clowns** *huddle —*
many ideas —

which conflict —
fights —
the sands of **Molereasons'** *timer have run out.*

Weasel (*from in the huddle*) Make it about Petersfield, and Peef, and the girl and all that!

Molereasons Time's up. Test time. (*Swishes cane.*) The Galoshes of Fortune – Go! —

Puff A girl went into Petersfield, Petersfield or Peef –

Drippens Wearing nothing but a Leatersfield, a Leatersfield or leaf –

Weasel A butchers' boy, he waved his Beetersfield, his Beetersfield or Beef –

Pimple And she, she flashed her Teetersfields, her Teetersfields or Teef –

Puff He cried: 'I am in Luttersfield, in Luttersfield, in Luff' –

Pimple She slapped his face and said: 'Enuttersfield, Enuttersfield, ENOUGH!' –

Weasel She said: 'Don't make me Lattersfield, me Lattersfield, me laff' –

Pimple 'The way you dress is Nattersfield, is Nattersfield, is naff' –

Drippens He took a pinch of Snuttersfield, of Snuttersfield or Snuff –

Weasel Atchoo! (*Sneezes trousers off.*) and he was standing in the Buttersfield, the Buttersfield or Buff –

Puff Ahem! – They heard a Cottersfield, a Cottersfield or Cough –

Drippens A Policeman, truncheon ready them to Bottersfield or Boff –

Pimple They ran into a Cattersfield, a Cattersfield a Caff –

Weasel And said: 'Quick! we need a Battersfield, a Battersfield or Baff' –

Puff They were both from the Naughtiesfield, the Naughtiesfield or Norf – So they said Battersfield for Bartersfield, Laff for Larf, and Baff for Borf –

Pimple They were both in the Bartersfield, the Bartersfield, the Barf –

Drippens But coming up the Partersfield, the Partersfield or Parf –

Weasel The Constable with Handcuttersfields, Handcuttersfields, Handcuffs –

Pimple His bum as big as Puttersfields, as Puttersfields as Puff's! –

Puff *inflates his bottom to enormous size —*
Clowns *and* **Molereasons** *take cover —*
Puff's *bottom explodes —*
Clowns *cheer.*

Pimple 'I must fly, my Luttersfield, my Luttersfield, my Luff!' –

Weasel 'Stay, thou sprightly Fluttersfield, my Fluttersfield, my Fluff –
   I swear by my butcher's Knightersfield, my Knightersfield, my Knife –
   I want you for my Whiteasfield, my Whiteasfield, my Wife' –

Drippens But in the twinkling of a Snittersfield, a Snittersfield or Sniff –

Pimple She left him with an Ittersfield, an Ittersfield or 'IF . . .' –

Puff Which stayed inside his Chesterfield, his Chesterfield or Chest –

Clowns (*together*) Was there something more he could have done for Besterfield, for Besterfield or Best . . . ?

Molereasons Clowns I am jubilant! Full Marks! I shall see if I can find the Box of Sticky Gold Stars!

Clowns (*jubilating*) Hooray!

Molereasons (*darkening*) But just one minute . . . what about the Galoshes? Where were the Galoshes of Fortune? (*Fingering cane.*)

Clowns *huddle in fear.*

Molereasons Hmm? (*Bearing down on them with cane.*) Eh?

Clowns *brighten.*

Clowns You were wearing them all the time, Sir!

Molereasons *looks down —*
Sees the Galoshes he still has on —
He brightens —
Mass ecstasy.

Puff Is this a Happy Time, Sir?

Molereasons Yes!

Puff Well, there you are – you've had two.

End